Pursuing Social

MW00772174

Challenges arise when teachers seek to enact socially just instruction while navigating social, classroom, and school dynamics. This research-based, field-tested text offers an accessible process for successfully negotiating these dynamics to identify consequential inroads for making positive educational change. With a focus on ELA instruction, but applicable to other content areas, Lillge's clear framework offers a language for naming, and practical tools for navigating, those spaces where different frameworks for teaching and learning challenge teachers' ability to act on their commitments to teach for justice.

Throughout the book, readers meet teachers who show how they reframed challenges and identified opportunities to work with others within inequitable systems to enact more just and equitable teaching. These case studies in teachers' own words allow readers to analyze how context and classroom culture influence teachers' negotiation processes. Serving as more than thought-provoking exemplars of what to do, the case studies and spotlighted "application moments" also invite readers to reflect on their own negotiations in the fieldwork, classrooms, and professional learning communities where they teach and learn. Comprehensive and illuminating, this book is a vital resource for pre-service teachers, teacher educators, and novice teachers.

Danielle Lillge is Associate Professor of English at Illinois State University, USA.

Pursuing Social Justice in ELA

A Framework for Negotiating the Challenges of Teaching

Danielle Lillge

 Routledge
Taylor & Francis Group

NEW YORK AND LONDON

Cover image: © Danielle Lillge

First published 2023
by Routledge
605 Third Avenue, New York, NY 10158

and by Routledge
4 Park Square, Milton Park, Abingdon, Oxon, OX14 4RN

Routledge is an imprint of the Taylor & Francis Group, an informa business

Library of Congress Cataloging-in-Publication Data
A catalog record for this title has been requested

ISBN: 9780367681432 (hbk)
ISBN: 9780367679057 (pbk)
ISBN: 9781003134442 (ebk)

DOI: 10.4324/9781003134442

Typeset in Goudy
by KnowledgeWorks Global Ltd.

To Joan and Gene, for introducing me to the rewards of sticking point negotiation before I had words to explain what you lived by example

Contents

Biography

Danielle Lillge is an Associate Professor in the Department of English at Illinois State University where she coordinates the Master's in English Education degree program with an emphasis in socially just English Language Arts instruction.

Foreword

In a recent book, *We Want to Do More Than Survive*, Dr. Bettina Love (2019) explains that:

> If we are honest, most dark suffering goes unnoticed by too many Americans, but America's educational history is overrun with dark suffering. Native American boarding schools, school segregation, English-only instruction, *Brown v. Board of Education*, No Child Left Behind, school choice, charter schools, character education, Race to the Top… all have been components of an educational system built on the suffering of students of color. I call this the educational survival complex, in which students are left learning to merely survive, learning how schools mimic the world they live in, thus making schools a training site for a life of exhaustion. (p. 27)

As a white, middle-class female preservice teacher in 1980, I knew little of that history, of that dark suffering. For the sakes of my students, I had to learn, and did, from outstanding mentors and extensive study. But let's imagine a group of young people—white, black, and brown—at this historical moment, where inequity is highly visible and openly named—who aspire to become ELA teachers in order to disrupt these patterns of systemic injustice. What if these aspiring educators know some of the painful history recounted by Dr. Love, and still believe wholeheartedly that literacies—speaking, writing, listening, reading—can be tools for liberation? What can our profession offer to support these future teachers so they can traverse this complicated landscape and begin making a difference without adding to the harm?

Danielle Lillge's *Pursuing Social Justice in ELA: A Framework for Negotiating the Challenges of Teaching* provides a framework and toolkit for exactly this purpose. This book offers "no magic beans," but instead honors the voices of preservice teachers and their contemporary dilemmas. These mini-cases, woven through each chapter and revisited collectively, form a foundation for the development and exploration of a stance toward literacy work that is humble, realistic, and ultimately transformative. By attending to what Dr. Lillge terms "sticking points"—moments where differing frameworks challenge a teacher's ability to act, first identifying and describing them, and eventually, determining whether, when, and how to act upon that dissonance—preservice (and practicing) teachers can learn to enact socially just instruction.

Pursing Social Justice in ELA, organized into three parts, begins by introducing two key concepts, "sticking points," and "frameworks," as well as demonstrating the way each chapter is structured. The predictability of the chapter formats, from the handmade drawings, the students' "In their own words" sections, as well as the "Apply your understanding" and "Reflecting" boxes, make the book highly useful in methods or student teaching seminar classes. The approach described in this book is one I wish I had encountered earlier in my career, because it is invaluable and nuanced.

I began to understand the power of interactional discourse analysis on literacy practice first through the work of the Santa Barbara Classroom Discourse Group, led by Dr. Judith Green, and then, through the presence of Dr. Lesley Rex, a member of that group, who eventually taught at University of Michigan. Dr. Rex and I collaborated to establish the Michigan Classroom Discourse Group for practicing educators involved in a local National Writing Project (NWP) site, the Oakland (MI) Writing Project. Dr. Rex is Danielle Lillge's mentor and friend.

In the context of regular Saturday meetings, educators collected transcripts from their classroom contexts and learned about what Michael Agar termed "rich points" (1994). Agar was talking about cultural dissonance—moments when people recognized they weren't working from the same meanings or cultural frames. The idea really was brought home for practicing teachers when they learned about a motto introduced by an experienced English teacher, David McEachen, to his students: "If anything is odd, inappropriate, confusing or boring, it's probably important." Lesley Rex and David McEachen wrote about this motto and the classroom culture it inspired in a 1999 *Research in the Teaching of English* article. Over weeks, months, and years, members of the discourse group described how those concepts and sayings began to help them approach challenging moments, conflicts, or "sticking points," as Danielle Lillge names them, with curiosity, with inquiry, and with patience. What was also notable was the way many group members, step by step, year by year, took on the struggle for justice more visibly.

Several became organizers against gun violence. Others engaged in carefully planned classroom projects and wrote books on youth voice and agency, on race and writing. One of Lillge's close collaborators, Linda Denstaedt, a discourse group member, went on to co-develop NWP's College, Community, and Career Writing Program, and co-wrote *Doing and Making Authentic Literacies* (2014) with me.

In *Pursuing Social Justice in ELA*, Dr. Lillge has taken ideas and practices from interactional discourse analysis (notetaking, notemaking, ethnographic observation) and distilled them to their essence through iterative work with young educators. I am impressed by what this short book contains. It's quietly radical in the sense that civil rights organizer Ella Baker described: "I use the term radical in its original meaning—getting down to and understanding the root cause. It means facing a system that does not lend itself to your needs and devising means by which you change that system." By showing young educators how to engage in "radical listening," Danielle Lillge provides signposts on a path toward liberatory education.

Dr. Laura Roop
Director, Western Pennsylvania Writing Project
University of Pittsburgh

References

Agar, M. (1994). *Language shock: Understanding the culture of conversation.* William Morrow.

Denstaedt, L., Roop, L. J., & Best, S. (2014). *Doing and making authentic literacies.* National Council of Teachers of English.

Love, B. L. (2019). *We want to do more than survive: Abolitionist teaching and the pursuit of educational freedom.* Beacon Press.

Rex, L. A., & McEachen, D. (1999). "If anything is odd, inappropriate, confusing, or boring, it's probably important": The emergence of inclusive academic literacy through English classroom discussion practices. *Research in the Teaching of English, 34*(1), 65–129

Acknowledgements

Over twenty years ago when I took my first teaching job, I was gladly welcomed into a community of colleagues who lived the joys of sticking point negotiation and created space where I could grow my understanding of and appreciation for what collegial collaboration can yield. Brenda Koprowski, Sandy Olszewski, Gini Pohlman, and David Roloff, thank you for incubating my belief that language is a site for social justice, schools a place of possibility in the hands of those committed to enacting change, and English classrooms a vision of democratic engagement.

To my editor Karen Adler, thank you for seeing the need for a book such as this that features processes which support teachers' ingenuity and commitment to enacting the socially just ELA. I am grateful that with your support, pre-service and beginning teachers have a book about how to negotiate the inevitable challenges that arise when they work toward enactment of their visions for tomorrow with others.

This book would also not have been possible were it not for the generosity of the case teachers featured throughout this book. When I shared your stories and narratives with others as I was drafting each chapter, readers were amazed at the strength of your candor, humility, inquisitiveness, and tenacious commitment to socially just ELA instruction, even as you recognized the complex and inequitable systems where that work finds wings and vision in your example. They celebrated that yours were stories of reality, including the uncertainty of next steps. Although I cannot name you, I wish to acknowledge how through your words, stories, and negotiation, you are inspiring possibilities for others.

I am similarly indebted to a group of veteran teacher leaders and consultants with the Oakland Writing Project who shared their experiences with and deepened my understandings about the power of sticking point negotiation as a sustaining practice through their ongoing work and learning with colleagues. Leah Barnett, Peter Haun, Katie Locano, and Laura Mahler, in the quiet of your everyday teaching and coaching, you epitomize what it looks like to open opportunities for colleagues' learning and teaching by studying your own discursive practices. You have taught me so much. I hope this book shines a light on your interactional gifts.

To the teacher candidates with whom I have worked and, importantly, learned, thank you for your willingness to allow me to experiment with these ideas in your company, to raise a perplexed eyebrow when things didn't make sense, and to generously honor your mentors and instructors as you grappled with sticking points that helped us all contemplate the challenges of enacting socially just instruction from your position as pre-service teachers who work within the frameworks and structures of others' teaching. When I reflect, as I often do, on what it means to our field and your students that you are the careful crafters of small instructional experiments, radical listeners, inquirers, and negotiators, there will always be a hopeful tomorrow.

I am grateful to the many colleagues who generously offered feedback as I journeyed forward in the writing of this book. Melinda McBee Orzluk, thank you for walking with me. Raquel Armas, Josie Maul, Abigail Byrnside, and Eliana Ladas, your comments, connections, and wonderings, especially as beginning and early career teachers helped ground my thinking about what matters most to those who will influence the next generation of student scholars. You motivate me to share this work with others so that you can find space to enact the change inspiring teaching you dream. Brooklyn Vogel and Shannon Maney-Magnuson, thank you for your eagerness to offer your insights and questions. You are mentors, instructors, and colleagues extraordinaire. Amy Knowles, your example of what it means to enact socially just field instruction deserves a book unto itself. Thank you for sharing your story with me. Your way of making complexity accessible inspired the "real life" sticking point negotiation anecdotes in this book. Maggie Morris Davis, your willingness to think with me about how to make sticking point negotiation more accessible to others has enriched each chapter. I am grateful for your support and encouragement in all forms. To live each day with the benefits of your programmatic vision for socially just ELA teacher education challenges me to grow in my own ability to live what I write. Linda Denstaedt, if ever there were an example of what it means to dig in and work alongside teachers to grow shared practice and language over time, not as drive by professional triage but as a sustainable model for ongoing professional learning, you are the real deal. Living together in schools with you continues to renew and inspire the work on these pages.

The whole notion of sticking point negotiation found roots in my earlier research, which benefitted from the questions and support of mentor scholars Anne Ruggles Gere, Mary Juzwik, and Megan Sweeney. Thank you for inviting me to define, rewrite, and clarify my understandings and arguments so that my scholarship could speak to diverse audiences, including most especially the unsung teachers who are on the ground agents of educational change through their commitments to teach for justice. Among those mentors, Lesley A. Rex, how eternally grateful I am that I found my way to the gifts of your scholarship, example, encouragement, questions, and conversation. You inspire me to be the mentor you've been to me for others: one who helps others negotiate their own sticking points through radical listening and inquiry. I hope in some small way that this book honors the lineage of my academic roots.

My familial roots remind me that this is a book that I've been drafting for more years than I knew. To Philip, thank you for reminding me through our conversations about the need for sticking point negotiation in all facets of life. I strive toward radical listening more than is likely evident. To Terry, you've taught me so much about teaching as relational work. My teaching and scholarship are stronger because you, too, value the ability to think and rethink how we work within inequitable systems to open possibilities for all students' learning and, in turn, living joyfully. You are my thinking partner in all ways. To Eleanor and Grant, thank you for reminding me about the possibilities of genuine inquiry that speaks from the heart to address the world's needs—small and large. You motivate my drive to build bridges.

Part I
Orientations

That you are here reading this book suggests that you believe in the potential of your own ability to teach for justice. That's so important, it's worth repeating in slightly different terms. You are the change. You are the possibility. What an exhilarating prospect!

Making the incredibly powerful choice to become a teacher who is committed to socially just instruction requires a willingness to grapple with a perplexing conundrum. Schools thrive because of brilliant possibilities: students and teachers who see and believe in their potential to nurture the future and contribute to more just and democratic communities. You likely already bring important ideas about how you will or already are teaching in ways that are socially just. You've read, begun learning, and contemplated how to go about teaching for justice.

At the same time, you are likely reading this book with the understanding that as you work to enact socially just instruction you, and other teachers like you who share similar commitments, will encounter challenges. After all, educational change and progress can feel incredibly slow and messy. Schools can perpetuate systems of inequity that preclude students from

DOI: 10.4324/9781003134442-1

reaching their potential and prevent, at times, teachers from affecting the change they desire.

How, then, you may wonder, do I find consequential inroads to affect change and teach for justice?

This book offers a set of possibilities for negotiating the inevitable challenges we face as we work to affect change in the everyday places of possibility where we teach and learn: English language arts (ELA) classrooms and professional learning communities. The beauty of our work as ELA teachers hinges on relational work with others: students, colleagues, mentor teachers, field instructors, families, administrators, support staff, community leaders, and the larger institutions to which we belong. Together, we'll explore an interactional process for learning to negotiate and reframe the challenges we face so that we can improve the educational opportunities for learners for whom conditions are unfair, inequitable, and unjust. Moreover, we'll learn how to work with colleagues to enact more just and equitable ELA instruction that benefits all learners.

Be forewarned. There are no magic beans here, no simple, sure proof solutions. Taking up the work of socially just teaching and learning can require extra, complicated work. Yet, that's likely why you're here, too. You know that already. You may (secretly or not so secretly) like a challenge. What we'll explore then is how we engage in the critical work of enacting socially just ELA instruction by negotiating challenges, or more specifically what we'll define as sticking points, so that we find energy and renewal in the opportunities our actions and interactions make possible. Engaging in the process of negotiation, you'll learn about as you read on, offers a way of remaining committed to teaching for justice in the face of perplexing conundrums. This book offers a skillset for working with and in relation to others, including systems of inequity, to create possibility in your everyday teaching and learning, schools and communities, students' lives, and the heartbeat of your professional life.

1

Embracing Sticking Points: Resources for Enacting Socially Just Instruction

Like many pre-service teachers, Alex is committed to instruction that opens opportunities for all students' learning. She is eager to jump into her fieldwork, so that she can apply her understandings about what socially just English language arts (ELA) instruction looks like. In the field, things feel "real." Identifying as a white, cisgender female who grew up in a major metropolitan area, Alex spends a lot of time talking about and reflecting on the value of including diverse lived experiences, histories, and texts in her classroom instruction.

Alex's fieldwork occurs in a suburban high school not unlike the one she attended. Of the nearly 2000 students who attend the school, half identify as white, 40% Hispanic, and the remaining 10% of the population as multiracial, Asian, or Black. Approximately a quarter of the student population is eligible for free or reduced lunch, and just under 10% of students are English language learners. The school dedicates time to, as Alex describes,

DOI: 10.4324/9781003134442-2

"professional learning about equity and identifying ways in which [teachers] can create inclusive spaces in classrooms." English teachers "consistently talk about culturally responsive teaching and socially just instruction specifically in terms of text selection and assignments to reach a broader range of students."

Aligned with the English department's commitment to infuse at least 15 minutes of daily independent, choice reading into each class, Alex's mentor teacher encourages her to book talk in their ninth grade courses. In her book selections, Alex seeks to promote "voices from historically marginalized writers," especially "authors of color." She designs a series of assessment tasks, or "pathways," from which students can choose to evidence thinking about their choice reading. Among the pathway opportunities, students may "write an alternate ending" to the text, "create a book trailer, write about the characters, or write an online book review." In her mind, the most substantial opportunity she offers is an invitation for students to become "an advocate" by "selecting a social justice issue" that their text explores, and then in consultation with Alex, developing a way of raising awareness about that issue with "an authentic audience."

After students have completed the choice reading assignment, Alex reflects on the pathways that students chose to pursue:

☞ 1.1 Alex, in her own words

The students in our classes come from a number of different middle schools. I gave students an introductory survey at the beginning of the semester to get to know them better. The different kinds of choices I designed came from what I knew about students. Most were really busy with extracurriculars. Some of them really liked writing. A lot of them liked being artistic. They spend a lot of time on social media. I knew some even entered a film contest every single summer. From this knowledge, I designed specific choices to include things that would be of interest to students and help them connect to the content of their reading. I think the assessment choices say a lot about the connections I was building with students.

I also want students to have choice in what they read. They ultimately got to pick a book they wanted to read. In my book talks, I wanted to model talk about systemic inequities. A few times a week, I would have conversations and ask students to fill the class in on what they were reading to model how to put texts into conversation with one another.

In the end, only one student chose the advocacy project option. I thought it was extremely powerful. After reading Angie Thomas's (2017) *The Hate U Give*, the student chose to raise awareness about police brutality. It's not frequently discussed in this predominately white, wealthier area of the suburbs. He had two poster boards, and on one he just had the names of victims of police brutality who have unfortunately lost their lives. And he just held that up there and stood in silence after asking his fellow students to read it. And then he had another board that had more information and statistics to define police brutality and who is typically targeted, which invited students to discuss further the issue. It was the biggest example I saw of students discussing systemic inequities. Even just one was exciting to see.

I wish, though, I had seen more students select the advocacy project to take up an issue related to social justice of some kind. I knew that it wasn't going to be too widespread, since students had free choice to self-select their reading. I had a lot of students choose romance YA [Young Adult Literature], for example, versus other suggestions I [offered in book talks] that might have dug deeper into issues of equity and injustice, although some romances do, too.

Sticking Points

Generative Resources for Professional Learning

In this excerpt, Alex shares what bubbled up during her fieldwork with students. Her description offers an example of a **sticking point**, a moment when differing frameworks challenge a teacher's ability to act. In the day-to-day of teaching and learning, sticking points are commonplace. As teachers—beginning *and* veteran—work to enact socially just instruction, sticking points emerge naturally. They emerge not just in interactions with students but also in other professional places too: the curriculum we teach, interactions with colleagues or others in our schools and professional learning spaces, the school districts and policies to which we are beholden, and so on. To understand *why* sticking points matter and *what* to do about them, teachers need to understand *what* they are and *how* they emerge.

Sticking points are byproducts of dissonance between two or more frameworks that differently define the purpose of learning, and by extension, teaching. A **framework** is a big picture orientation to how individuals and groups of people define the work at hand. Frameworks act as umbrellas that house a number of understandings, which inform decisions. They help people—not just teachers—make decisions all the time. In people's everyday lives, frameworks inform decisions about what to wear, which way to get to school or work most efficiently, with whom to (and not to) engage in lengthier conversations, and how much time to devote to particular tasks. In our teaching lives, frameworks inform decisions about, among other things, what to teach, when to teach what, how to teach that, how to teach these students, and why we teach what we teach.

No matter where you are in your journey as a teacher, you employ and draw upon frameworks for ELA instruction. Even as we sit in other instructors' classrooms, we are thinking about and employing frameworks to make meaning of what we're seeing and experiencing. To surface these frameworks, explore one of the following invitations:

- Think about a single instructional choice you have made in your recent teaching or rehearsal of teaching. It may have been something quite simple like choosing to chat with a student about that student's weekend plans before class begins. Or it might have been a choice that required advanced planning such as deciding to open the discussion of a text by asking students to share their confusion. Once you've identified a single choice, reflect on why that choice mattered to you. What were you attempting to accomplish with that choice? Why did you select that instructional choice rather than others that might have been available to you? What did you hope that choice messaged to students about your role, their learning, and their role in the classroom community you were seeking to foster?
- Think about someone else's teaching you have recently observed or experienced. Identify one instructional move that the teacher made during the lesson. Reflect on what that choice seemed to message to you about the teacher's rationale for action. What did that instructional choice seem to accomplish? In other words, what in your mind, was the goal of that instructional choice? What did that choice message to you about the kind of instruction and, in turn, learning that matters to that teacher?

Your answers to these questions begin to name framework commitments that motivate and inform your own ELA teaching. In this book I, a fellow teacher, focus on our daily lives as teachers who develop or adopt frameworks for socially just instruction that inform our everyday instructional decisions. However, as your reflections and experiences likely affirm, there are different and overlapping frameworks for teaching and ELA instruction that also circulate.

Surfacing frameworks can, at least at first, be challenging. Most often, we draw on framework understandings to make decisions automatically, and we don't need to think about them much when things go smoothly in our teaching and everyone seems to be working toward a similar goal.

When things don't go as planned or as we anticipate they should, however, we experience a **clash** between frameworks. Clashes, or sticking points, bring our attention to frameworks and how they influence our actions, because we have to make decisions about whether and how to negotiate them.[1]

The Ant Interlude

We'll return to Alex later, but first let me share a story that my friend Amy tells, which illustrates well how sticking points emerge naturally.

One spring day, Amy noticed ants in her kitchen. Since it was not uncommon for ants to find their way inside each spring, Amy drew on her framework understandings for how to eradicate them. She concocted a home remedy and spritzed it around the exterior walls of her kitchen. Then, she waited. Past experience had taught her that in no more than a few weeks of this patterned response, the ants would be gone.

When they didn't disappear, she mentioned the struggle to her partner who listened well. Amy pleaded for help: "Can you please call an exterminator to see how we can get rid of these ants?" A few weeks later when no exterminator had appeared and with the ant population on the rise, Amy revisited the conversation with her partner before a scheduled trip. "I'm going away for the weekend. Can you please have an answer from the exterminator when I return?" When Amy returned, the ants remained. Her partner had not contacted the exterminator. Overhearing the conversation, their son said, "I was watching a TV show about carpenter ants. Do you think these are carpenter ants?" Without much pause, Amy's partner phoned the exterminators.

Amy's partner did not seem too concerned about the presence of ants in the kitchen until their son's question evoked an entirely different framework for the problem at hand. Before that point, Amy's urgency reflected different framework understandings about the severity of the situation and the associated need for action. When her partner considered the prospect of these potential carpenter ants eating through their home, a new framework prompted immediate action. (And, for the record, it was a good thing. They *were* carpenter ants.)

Resources for Determining How to Respond

What on earth, you may say, does this ant story have to do with my teaching?

If we understand learning, and therefore teaching, as a socially co-constructed process, then sticking points prompt us to notice and carefully reflect on the frameworks that inform our shared learning with others. Sticking points raise the question, "Are we really on the same page here?"

In Amy's case, she believed that she and her partner shared a framework for understanding the trouble with ants in the kitchen. After their son's comment, though, she realized that she and her partner did not in fact share framework understanding. The dissonance explained why her partner had failed to act in response to her urgings and why he had eagerly acted when their son's comments framed the problem differently. What Amy's experience also makes visible is that being able to identify sticking points helps us carefully weigh how to act in response.

Being able to determine whether, when, why, and how to act is a critical teaching skill, too. Noticing and then negotiating sticking points helps us accomplish what might otherwise seem overwhelming. As you read this book, you will develop the skills that enable we teachers to respond in-the-moment and over time to the constantly evolving realities of our professional work. The following features will support this goal:

- Look for the boxes with this symbol: ☞. These are places where we will hear directly from case study teachers **in their own words**. Case study teachers' use of the skills you'll learn in this book enables them to negotiate sticking points in support of socially just instruction.
- You'll find opportunities to try out these skills by applying them to your on-going fieldwork in diverse classrooms. To be sure, by diverse here I mean a wide range of classrooms wherein we teachers consider student populations within that school as well as individual student's identity markers and how they influence students' experience of schooling. These identity markers might include but not be limited to race, ethnicity, class, gender, sexual orientation, religion or spirituality, ability, nationality, citizenship, and language. For the purposes of this book and our work as ELA teachers, considering diverse schools might also include examining each school's geographical location and characteristics of the communities it serves, especially in the ways that

those characteristics and locations make that school unique and distinct from other schools. Look for these **application moments** in invitations flagged with this symbol: ☑. Often, application moments include invitations to share your thinking and efforts with a colleague. By design, sharing your application efforts with colleagues provides an opportunity to enact the process as you go and with others.

- Because research tells us that we all solidify our learning through reflection, you'll also discover opportunities to **reflect on your application** efforts through-out the book where you find this symbol: ✐.[2]

- Finally, throughout the book you'll find my hand drawn **sketches** that serve an important function in the text as well. Taking up the work of sticking point negotiation, like socially just ELA instruction, may at times feel com-plicated or even inaccessible without more extensive experience, especially if you assume you must or will master the skills we'll learn before trying them out. The sketches offer visually accessible ways of understanding the key skills, or moves, for trying out and evolving our understanding of sticking negotiation. They offer entry points, then. Their imperfectness by design can serve as a quick reminder that the process we'll be learning and trying out benefits most from a willingness to honor that the goal is not perfection or rightness. Rather, our goal is to embrace the process, even as we're learning it, in order to strengthen our understanding of what it yields in our own teaching and, importantly, in the learning experiences we seek to contribute to and foster in our classrooms and professional learning spaces.

Alex: Case Study

For a glimpse into the process we'll unpack throughout the book, let's return to Alex who we met earlier in this chapter. Her awareness that sticking points could emerge in her teaching enabled her to notice when one did emerge. Her sticking point surfaced when she realized that although she had framed students' choice reading options to invite conversations about what Cindy O'Donnell-Allen (2011) refers to as "tough texts," providing students with completely open choice meant that students chose texts that might not have lent themselves as easily to conversations about or exploration of social injustices. So, although Alex framed her book talks and some assessment choices as invitations into conversations with and about texts that required students to grapple with and deepen their understanding of social injustices and inequities, students understood the assessment work as prioritizing their freedom of choice.

☑ **1.2 Apply your understanding**

Now it's your turn to reflect on where you see the potential for teaching sticking points in your own fieldwork. As you think about previous field experiences, current fieldwork site, or upcoming future fieldwork, what do you know about the students, classroom, or school that might potentially pose sticking points in your work or teaching there? Why do you think these realities posed or might pose sticking points for you?

As you are likely already aware and thinking, simply identifying sticking points does not help you fully address them. However, as Alex's case makes clear, without a fine-tuned ability to notice sticking points and, equally important, understand where they are coming from, we teachers cannot respond carefully and thoughtfully in ways that help us maintain productive professional relationships with students and colleagues. Therefore, sticking points also prompt us to explore, "How can I invite others onto the same page here?"

Alex's sticking point presented her with a dilemma as she worked to enact socially just instruction: How best to respond? She wanted to navigate the sticking point, especially because she knew that she would be running another cycle of choice reading. Choosing how to navigate the sticking point meant carefully reflecting on a set of related considerations. On one hand, aware of research that supports the necessity of developing students' readerly identities, Alex wanted to promote independent, choice reading (Buehler, 2016). She wanted students to find pleasure in reading and discover meaningful ways of authentically engaging in talk about texts (Wilhelm & Smith, 2016). And, listening to her talk, she had every reason to believe that she was accomplishing these goals.

☞ **1.3 Alex, in her own words**

At the end of all this, after all the assignments were due, I did another survey. I asked for some feedback, since this was a brand-new assignment that I designed. A lot of students really liked the amount of choices. I thought that they would be overwhelming, but they really liked the options. Students favored the artistic options the most. A lot of them liked having a range of options.

On many levels, Alex could well have taken this student feedback as a green light to continue on in the same way moving forward. Students were pleased with the choices in texts and in assessment pathways. They were engaged, and they were enthusiastic about the opportunities. What teacher wouldn't be content with these outcomes?

Still, Alex's framework for socially just ELA instruction coupled with the fact that "only one student chose the advocacy" option posed a sticking point in her mind. Choice was an important component of a socially just classroom for Alex. Nonetheless, she wanted to nudge students toward "tough texts" that would lend themselves to critical conversations about injustices and inequities, especially in their reading about those whose lived experiences differed from their own. The sticking point for Alex arose from the fact that students could easily participate and make choices that effectively enabled them to sidestep tough texts and talk.

As Alex reflected on why this was, she found herself critically considering a set of factors that influenced how she designed the independent, choice reading text selection and assessment pathways. It was early in the school year, and Alex was eager to develop meaningful professional relationships with students and promote a classroom community where students felt valued and important in the class's socially constructed learning. Additionally, she was aware of her role as a guest in her mentor teacher's classroom, even though he was incredibly welcoming and made many efforts to position her as an equal, especially in their work with students. She admired his instructional approaches and appreciated that even though they did not always "share the same language" to talk about how they were committed to "socially just instruction," she could "see it in action" in his classroom. When it came to text selection, she explained that her mentor teacher "has a lot of books in his room, so a lot of the books we chose were based off of his classroom library." They both had "a hand in [student] selections," because they both

---

☑ **1.4 Apply your understanding**

Extending your thinking from Box 1.2, think about a teaching sticking point you have already experienced in the field or one you could imagine experiencing in a field classroom. Describe the sticking point. What considerations flash through your mind as you think about responding? How are those considerations based on what you know about the content and context of your teaching, as they were in Alex's case?

"book talk a lot of books." She chuckled as she explained, "We always joke because we have very different tastes in books. I love YA, and he doesn't really love YA as much. He loves mystery-thriller. I feel like a lot of my suggestions were more focused on social justice issues." Alex's reflections highlight her efforts to consider the set of content and contextual factors that shape our understanding of sticking points.

Through her reflections, Alex makes visible *that* our ELA teaching requires careful negotiation of sticking points. As a reader of this book, you likely already agree that learning to enact socially just instruction is not as simple as acknowledging that sticking points will occur. There's an important difference between knowing that sticking points exist and knowing how to negotiate them. Because you're interested in learning *how* to negotiate sticking points, you are likely wondering:

- How did Alex's framework for socially just ELA teaching and learning enable her to notice the emergence of a sticking point?
- How did Alex's ability to name the complex factors at work in her instructional decision-making enable her to identify possibilities for negotiating the sticking point?
- How did Alex work to maintain positive relationship with her mentor teacher as a guest in his classroom culture and within a larger school system so that she could continue to develop her ability to enact socially just ELA instruction?
- What, ultimately, did she decide to do?

Book Overview

Cases

In the chapters that follow, we'll explore these questions by examining the experiences, or cases, of Alex and other teachers who are committed to socially just ELA instruction. I've learned from these teachers through my research with them in ELA classrooms and professional development spaces (Lillge, 2015, 2019a, 2019b; Lillge & Dominguez, 2017; Lillge & Knowles, 2020). They exemplify what it means to deeply engage in the intellectual work of teaching and professional learning. Their engagement begins with an assumption that teaching is always draft work (Juzwik et al., 2013). Teachers, like all learners, are always in a state of becoming. Therefore, the teachers you'll meet embrace a self-reflexive eagerness to read and analyze their classroom interactions and instructional decisions. Their willingness to share their thinking and experiences in-progress offer an opportunity to learn from and alongside them.

A Transferrable Framework for Negotiating Sticking Points

In my role as a secondary ELA teacher in rural, suburban, and urban class-rooms, literacy coach, and now teacher educator, it sometimes surprises the beginning teachers with whom I am grateful to learn when I say, "There's no way you will know everything or be able to anticipate all that might arise in your future teaching." Teaching is people work. As such, it is deeply connected to the classrooms where we interact with students and colleagues. Therefore, we will never be able to fully predict or proactively plan for every unexpected interaction or event. Giving voice to this reality can, under-standably, make us feel awash in a sea of uncertainty. It can make us fear the unexpected aspects of our work and instead seek to avoid them at the expense of our commitment to socially just instruction.

This book offers a different way of responding. Rather than fearing the unforeseen, we teachers can find assurance in our ability to rehearse and, therefore, strengthen a process for navigating and negotiating the unex-pectedly inevitable, so that when sticking points do occur, we can read the moment and respond thoughtfully. Learning that process will enable you to adapt and adjust over time by transferring your ability to negotiate sticking points to different classroom and professional interactions.

Social and Interactional Power to Affect Change

Transferring your ability to negotiate sticking points to new interactions is contingent upon understanding that power is an inevitable part of all social situations, including, of course, our professional interactions. In this book, we'll explore power from a social and cultural lens. From that perspective, power is defined as the ability to maneuver in social situations and interac-tions in ways that enable people to be seen and heard as they desire. Power is a social conduit by which people feel agentive in articulating and achiev-ing their goals and identities. Viewing power this way helps to illuminate how people can share power and how power can circulate rather than pop-ular conceptions of power as something that someone has all or nothing of. Rather, in this book, taking this interactional view of power can help us con-sider how we might circulate power within classrooms and other professional interactions (Rex & Schiller, 2009). As teachers, in our social interactions with others—whether students or colleagues or anyone else we interact with professionally, we can use our power as a resource for considering how we can feel agentive in enacting the instruction we are committed to while also carefully considering our relationship with others in order to help them exercise their power, too. Thus, power is a part of the dynamic of working in relationship to and with others.

For beginning teachers, especially, navigating power dynamics can feel tricky. After all, there will be times when teachers must recognize their limited power to enact instructional framework commitments. Take, for example, interactions with a mentor teacher. Let's take as given that all mentors wish to support you in your professional journey. They have different kinds of power than you do in the school system and classroom where you may be a guest or early career teacher. They may, understandably and commendably, see the exercise of their knowledge and expertise on your behalf and on behalf of the school as a way of supporting your growth and learning through their role as a mentor. A mentor's interjection during your teaching, for instance, might be their way of evidencing their knowledge and redirecting students toward your learning goals. It may not necessarily feel that way to you as you desire to take up the work of teaching with increasing independence and navigate unexpected interactions in-the-moment while later reflecting on them with your mentor. However, understanding what power is and how it works for your mentor (or any other person with whom you interact professionally, including students) and for you can help you read, reread, and then respond to the situation at hand. Doing so can enable your mentor to continue to exercise their power while also enabling you to carve out space for instructional experimentation thus enabling you to exercise your power in the space, too.

In short, knowing how power works can help you identify your own agency to affect instructional change in support of student learning. At times, that understanding may lead you to conclude that it is more advantageous to lay low and wait until you can identify a better time or space to act. The choice to lay low can feel uncomfortable and difficult, because waiting can feel like you're compromising your ability to act in support of what you believe in. As we journey through the text and explore the cases of other beginning and veteran teachers to see how they navigate such power dynamics, we'll consider how seeing spaces of interactional tension that result from these power dynamics as opportunities can help us successfully navigate sticking points and, importantly, preserve relationships.

Contextual Applicability

To be clear, though, this is not a traditional case study book. Often the inclusion of case studies in education books invite readers to contemplate, "What would you do if you were in this situation?" Or, "Imagine you're here." While valuable, this approach neglects the ways contexts require specific kinds of responsive instruction. Considering case studies for their universality can obscure how teachers work within the particular contexts where they teach by reading and responding to ever evolving understandings of people, places, interactional dynamics, and systems.

By contrast, cases in this book offer a transferrable process for reading context-based interactions as a necessary part of negotiating sticking points. Approached this way, I hope the cases in this book help you inhabit, rehearse, and reflect on a *process* for negotiating sticking points in the context(s) where you are learning to enact socially just instruction. Successful adoption of this process relies on your ability to draw on contextual knowledge in order to act. In each chapter, you will find opportunities to analyze how the context and classroom culture in particular cases influence teachers' negotiation processes. Beyond analysis that unpacks the process, each chapter invites you to try out and reflect on the process in your unique field-based teaching context in order to further strengthen your ability to read and respond to the learning cultures you are a part of and to which you contribute.

Part I

Socially Just ELA Lens

The ability to identify sticking points is also predicated on a clear understanding of and ability to articulate an evolving framework for socially just ELA. In Chapter Two, I distinguish frameworks for socially just ELA instruction from other frameworks for ELA teaching and learning to clarify the central focus on socially just instruction and sticking points in this book. Then, we'll explore the importance of defining and co-constructing with others frameworks for socially just teaching practice that undergird our instructional decision-making.

Interactional Focus

Chapter Two, therefore, also establishes another important thread throughout the book: its emphasis on social interactions as the primary vehicle by which we learn and negotiate sticking points. Since, there will always be sticking points associated with teacher efforts to enact socially just teaching practices, there will always be a need to talk with others about sticking points and the frameworks that inform shared instructional decision making.

Part II

In Part Two of the book, we'll unpack the sticking point negotiation process.

Zooming In

First, we'll explore how zooming in to carefully consider what's going on in classroom and learning interactions can help us notice and study sticking points. Chapter Three focuses on how to notice when, where, and how sticking points arise when frameworks clash. To understand how to respond to sticking points, we need a means of slowing classroom and professional interactions, so that we can analyze them. We'll learn how notetaking can serve as a tool for noticing. In Chapter Four, we learn about how to frame sticking point that we notice using the interpretative tool of notemaking. We'll explore in Chapter Five how notemaking can invite further inquiry into questions we raise about the nature of the sticking point and the interactions that inform our understanding of the learning culture where the sticking point has emerged. As we inquire, we can use radical listening as an important tool for seeking greater clarity about other's framework understandings.

Zooming Out

With the benefit of what we learn by zooming in, we can begin to zoom out and take stock of what we've learned before deciding whether and how to act on what we've learned. In Chapter Six, we will explore how these understandings help us consider others' and check our own perspectives as we work with others in support of common learning goals. Chapter Seven describes the necessity of naming the various frameworks at play in the sticking points we're investigating.

Together, these analytic efforts help us learn ways of later negotiating sticking points with and in relation to the individuals *and* systems of schooling we work within, including the systems of oppression we seek to redress. Without the ability to engage in naming and radical listening, we risk misinterpreting and misconstruing the nature of sticking points, including how our colleagues and mentors may share a commitment to socially just instruction but go about enacting it differently. Chapter Eight makes clear how our ability to negotiate sticking points is contingent on our ability to read how and why they emerge such that we can re-interpret or re-frame our understanding of sticking points. To act without naming and re-framing sticking points is to risk perpetuating the inequities and inequalities that we seek to disrupt through our teaching.

Part III

Taking Action

In Part Three, we'll consider when, where, and how to act on what we've learned about the sticking points in our teaching and professional interactions. The goal in doing so is to preserve and strengthen our relationships with students, mentors, and colleagues so that we can continue to enact and pursue socially just instruction. Chapter Nine offers strategies for discerning whether and how we wish to take action in response to a sticking point. The discursive tools in this chapter will help you respect cultural norms and others' frameworks, which requires careful balance between remaining open to possibilities for adjusting action plans in response to others' thoughts as well as ways of remaining true to your own evolving frameworks for socially just teaching practices.

Moving Forward

Understanding that sticking points are a normal and natural part of socially just ELA instruction affirms that they are not unique to the experiences of beginning teachers—something research also confirms.[3] In the final chapter, we will consider how the tools in the book prepare you for future efforts to enact socially just teaching practices and ongoing learning throughout your career by examining the cases of veteran teachers and their work to jointly explore sticking points. These teachers illustrate the power of collaborative professional communities that sustain socially just teaching practices and that enable teachers to affect change through their day-to-day interactions and instructional efforts.

Taken together, the chapters in this book illuminate how sticking points can become a powerful resource for developing adaptability and relational responsiveness to the commonplace realities of teaching and learning in diverse classrooms and in support of diverse learners. As one pre-service teacher candidate, Jax, reflected on their learning (see Box 1.5), sticking points offer compelling evidence for what's made possible when we embrace the negotiation process. Teachers who understand how to read and respond to sticking points need not spend their days fearful of what will happen when sticking points arise. Instead, as the teachers you'll meet affirm, with practice employing this negotiation process, sticking points become generative resources for strengthening our interactions, instruction, and ability to persist in support of all students' literacy learning.

 1.5 Jax, in their own words

I found sticking point negotiation to be very beneficial as it offered me an opportunity to explore what challenged me as a future socially just ELA teacher. I found that my understanding of sticking points deepened as I got to see how I can use these challenging moments to better myself not only as an educator but as a person as well.

 1.6 Reflecting

Considering what you've read in this chapter about where we're headed together, what questions do you hope your reading about and efforts to begin negotiating sticking points will help you explore or address on your journey to become a socially just ELA teacher?

Notes

1 For extended conversation about the normalcy of these clashes for pre-service teachers in particular, see Lillge and Knowles (2020).
2 There is a long-standing understanding that reflection supports teachers' ongoing professional learning (Cruickshank, 1987; Schön, 1983, 1987; Shulman, 2011), including scholarship that centers the work of reflection as interactional (Connell, 2014) and central to ELA teacher education (Harman et al., 2016; Smagorinsky et al., 2015; Vetter et al., 2017)
3 Research affirms that the prevalence of sticking points continues across teachers' careers, especially for those who are committed to socially just instruction (e.g., Kohli et al., 2015; Um, 2019; van der Want et al., 2018; Williamson, 2017).

References

Buehler, J. (2016). *Teaching reading with YA literature: Complex texts, complex lives.* National Council of Teachers of English.

Connell, M. T. (2014). Recovering the social dimension of reflection. *Journal of Catholic Education, 17*(2). https://doi.org/10.15365/joce.1702022014

Cruickshank, D. R. (1987). *Reflective teaching: The preparation of students of teaching.* Association of Teacher Educators.

Harman, R. M., Ahn, S., & Bogue, B. (2016). Reflective language teacher education: Fostering discourse awareness through critical performative pedagogy. *Teaching and Teacher Education, 59*, 228–238. https://doi.org/10.1016/j.tate.2016.06.006

Juzwik, M. M., Borsheim-Black, C., Caughlan, S., & Heintz, A. (2013). *Inspiring dialogue: Talking to learn in the English classroom.* Teachers College Press.

Kohli, R., Picower, B., Martinez, A., & Ortiz, N. (2015). Critical professional development: Centering the social justice needs of teachers. *International Journal of Critical Pedagogy, 6*(2), 7–24

Lillge, D. (2015). *When does literacy professional development work? Understanding how instructors learn to teach writing in their disciplinary classrooms* [Doctoral dissertation, University of Michigan]. Deep Blue. http://hdl.handle.net/2027.42/111474

Lillge, D. (2019a). Improving professional development relationships that support teacher learning. *English Teaching: Practice & Critique, 18*(3), 365–381. doi: https://doi.org/10.1108/ETPC-12-2018-0121.

Lillge, D. (2019b). Uncovering conflict: Why teachers struggle to apply professional development learning about the teaching of writing. *Research in the Teaching of English, 53*(4), 340–362

Lillge, D., & Dominguez, D. (2017). Launching lessons: Framing our approach to multicultural, multivoiced YA literature. *English Journal, 107*(1), 33–40

Lillge, D., & Knowles, A. (2020). Sticking points: Sites for developing capacity to enact socially just instruction. *Teaching and Teacher Education, 94*, 103098. https://doi.org/10.1016/j.tate.2020.103098

O'Donnell-Allen, C. (2011). *Tough talk, tough texts: Teaching English to change the world.* Heinemann.

Rex, L., & Schiller, L. (2009). *Using discourse analysis to improve classroom interaction.* Routledge.

Schön, D. A. (1983). *The reflective practitioner: How professionals think in action.* Basic Books.

Schön, D. A. (1987). *Educating the reflective practitioner: Toward a new design for teaching and learning in the professions.* Jossey-Bass.

Shulman, L. (2011). Knowledge and teaching: Foundations of the new reform. *Harvard Educational Review, 57*(1), 1–23. doi: https://doi.org/10.17763/haer.57.1.j463w79r56455411.

Smagorinsky, P., Shelton, S. A., & Moore, C. (2015). The role of reflection in developing eupraxis in learning to teach English. *Pedagogies: An International Journal*, *10*(4), 285–308. doi: https://doi.org/10.1080/1554480X.2015.1067146.

Thomas, A. (2017). *The hate u give*. Blazer & Bray.

Um, S. J. (2019). Politics of hybridity: Teaching for social justice in an era of standards-based reform. *Teaching and Teacher Education*, *81*, 74–83.

van der Want, A. C., Schellings, G. L. M., & Mommers, J. (2018). Experienced teachers dealing with issues in education: A career perspective. *Teachers and Teaching*, *24*(7), 802–824. doi: https://doi.org/10.1080/13540602.2018.1481024.

Vetter, A., Myers, J., Reynolds, J., Stumb, A., & Barrier, C. (2017). The daybook defense: How reflection fosters the identity work of readers and writers. *Journal of Adolescent & Adult Literacy*, *61*(1), 37–44. doi: https://doi.org/10.1002/jaal.643.

Wilhelm, J. D., & Smith, M. W. (2016). The power of pleasure reading: What we can learn from the secret reading lives of teens. *English Journal*, *105*(6), 25–30

Williamson, T. (2017). Listening to many voices: Enacting social justice literacy curriculum. *Teaching and Teacher Education*, *61*, 104–114. https://doi.org/10.1016/j.tate.2016.10.002

2
Navigating Sticking Points: Socially Just Frameworks as Compasses

The ability to negotiate sticking points requires clarity about the frameworks that inform our instructional decision-making. Without such clarity, it would be difficult to respond to sticking points in ways that are consistent with the kinds of instruction we aspire to enact. To understand why it can be challenging to respond without framework clarity, let's explore a useful analogy.

Learning to Drive

If you've learned to drive a vehicle, it's highly likely that you may have begun your studies in a classroom. There, you likely read about how to drive, learned about your responsibilities, and memorized rules and laws. You may also have watched some films of other people driving in order to learn from

DOI: 10.4324/9781003134442-3

their example. The tests you might have taken assessed your proficiency in understanding *about* how to drive.

For many of us who have learned to drive, though, the real test of our learning came as we began driving behind the wheel—as we began to put our understanding into action. Often, that driving occurred under the mentorship of an instructor who sat nearby to intervene by pushing the brake, if needed. At first, our efforts may well have been stilted and inconsistent.

I recall, for example, an instructor telling me to turn right at an intersection. I promptly turned left. Luckily, no one was harmed by my error.

Nonetheless, no one was more surprised than me about the error in my performance as I pulled to the side of the road and listened to the instructor question my decision-making. It all seemed so logical and obvious and confusing. I knew left from right. I knew the rules of the road. I knew I would need to make quick decisions based on what I had learned. Yet, putting all of this knowledge together as I drove for "real" in the company of a "real" audience was an entirely different challenge. If I'm honest, my ego did suffer a bit. Two of my peers watched and listened from the backseat.

Thankfully, I moved beyond my embarrassment. I tried and tried again. I made more mistakes, to be sure. But, eventually, with practice and feedback, I got better and better at making quick but informed decisions that required me to draw on what I knew about driving, about the places where I drove, and about how to read other drivers' decisions.

Eventually, I found my driving groove. It became easier, and there was an enjoyable flow that accompanied the ability to explore the unknown and embrace the unexpected. In fact, I came to enjoy the chance to travel to new places. Of course, encountering a roadblock or a construction site was an inevitable part of the journey, but I became much more adept at responding with patience and ease. The unexpected became an expected part of the journey, and it made the destination all the sweeter when I arrived.

Learning to Teach

Learning to teach in diverse classroom contexts is a lot like learning to drive. At first, we study others' examples and expertise. Often, we apply our learning in early teaching rehearsals of our lesson plans and unit design. We teach with peers and instructors who offer us feedback, which enables us to refine our understandings in relation to our practice.

The real test of our understanding, though, comes when we work to translate and adapt our learning within the field-based classrooms where we try out our teaching for the first time with "real" students. Like my very clear understanding of the difference between left and right, we may understand that socially just English language arts (ELA) instruction requires specific pedagogical content knowledge about how to engage students in disciplinary inquiry that also honors their out-of-school literacies, for example (Moje, 2007). But, when we begin teaching the lessons of our design, an unexpected student question or contribution can pose an unanticipated sticking point. We may respond in ways that are surprising, even to us.

What we do in response to these moments is of critical importance. Socially just ELA instruction requires us to meet new challenges through our teaching. After all, if we seek to prepare students to successfully negotiate challenges in their own learning and lives, we have to model our ability to do so, too.

If in these challenging moments, we seek the safety of what we have seen or done before, we risk reflexively following the standardized GPS of education, if you will, without considering whether the suggested or familiar route is our preferred choice. When we choose to rotely follow without carefully weighing what's at stake and for whom, we risk perpetuating the assumption that teaching as it has always been done or as we have seen it done is in the best interest of those involved in the challenge, including most especially the students in our classroom. Even more weighty, let's consider the implications of a choice to perpetuate the status quo. If we recognize that schools have historically preserved systems of inequity that disadvantage certain populations of students over others, a choice to circumvent the need to negotiate challenges can position us as complicit in the very systems of inequity we seek to transform through our everyday teaching and professional learning.

Alternately, with support from mentors and colleagues, we can see these challenges as sticking points. I use the word sticking points to emphasize their temporariness. Rather than more permanent assumptions about feeling and being stuck, sticking points are momentary pauses on the longer journey of and toward change. Choosing to see sticking points in this way opens opportunities to clarify the framework understandings that drive our eagerness to travel to new places in our teaching. Viewed this way, exploring the emergence of sticking points in our daily teaching can invite reflection on and refinement of the frameworks that undergird and inform our everyday teaching decisions. These frameworks offer us perpetual orientation and reorientation, a kind of compass for traveling into the unknown and worthwhile terrain of socially just ELA instruction.

Frameworks: Drivers of Instructional Decisions

Understanding how to negotiate sticking points depends upon knowing the frameworks that inform why the work of negotiation matters—what it supports or makes possible in our teaching. Frameworks guide our instructional choices. Much like the foundation of a building, which provides the building's most critical structural support, the frameworks that undergird our instructional decisions offer critical support for our instructional actions.

In order to understand how teaching frameworks are built, it is important to understand their relationship to **frames**. Erving Goffman (1974) defines a frame as a cognitive structure that develops as people work together within a particular context to interpret their interactions by answering the question, "What is it that's going on here?" (p. 8). Distinct from other views that prioritize individual cognition, Goffman's work emphasizes the social nature of how frames develop. Those scholars who build on Goffman's work, focus on how frames are actively co-constructed with and in relation to others, in the moment, and often indirectly as people infer the meaning of verbal and non-verbal interactions (Scheff, 2006; Tannen, 1993, 1998). Importantly, then, frames evolve in relation to ongoing interactions.

Cruz: Case Study

An example may help to clarify (see Box 2.1). During student teaching Cruz shares a story from the field.

☞ 2.1 Cruz, in his own words

Last week while I was teaching, one of the building administrators popped into our classroom. At first, I didn't notice, because students were totally engaged in their efforts to compose digital book talks. In our classroom, space is tight, so students were scattered all over the room. Some were sitting in and around desks. Others were at tables in the back of the room. Some were sitting on the carpeted section of the floor. The classroom was pretty lively and loud, but students were all focused on their collaboration. I was circling to conference with each group about their drafting when I noticed the administrator out the corner of my eye chatting with my mentor teacher at her desk. I didn't think anything of it. That admin. is pretty visible in the building and often pops in and out.

After the period was over, my mentor said that the admin. asked nonchalantly about the noise level in our class and my classroom management skills when she saw that I was the one teaching. I was grateful that my mentor said that students were just really engaged in the work they were doing. "That's the sign of focused students," she explained to the admin.

In this story, the building administrator questions Cruz's mentor teacher to understand whether the noise level in the classroom should be interpreted within the frame of poor classroom management or the frame of student engagement. To Cruz's relief, his mentor affirms that the noise level can and should be interpreted through the frame of student engagement, which is the welcome byproduct of the work Cruz has thoughtfully designed.

When frames coalesce under a larger overarching structure that offers a rationale for what it is that we are about in our ELA teaching, the overarching rationale is referred to as a **framework.** Thus, a framework includes a number of frames that join together in support of a common goal or purpose for ELA teaching and learning.

In Cruz's story, his mentor teacher shared the framework understanding that learning is socially accomplished through interactions with others. Therefore, a classroom that does not regularly invite lively and focused discussion and problem-solving, as was the case in the lesson that the administrator popped into, does not fulfill their framework commitments to fostering interactive opportunities for learning. In fact, the term classroom management doesn't align well with Cruz's framework for ELA teaching and learning, because management implies a need to control students and their behaviors. By contrast, Cruz's framework suggests a different goal: design meaningful classroom activities and discussions that invite student engagement. Rather than seeking to maintain compliance, engagement follows from teachers' efforts to design instruction that makes visible the relevance of learning within and beyond the classroom by positioning students as knowledgeable, capable thinkers, and speakers who contribute to and benefit from a community of learners. Student engagement is a frame that contributes to Cruz's larger framework for ELA teaching, which drives his decisions about how to engage students in meaningful ELA learning.

The Emergence and Evolution of Teaching Frameworks

As a noun, a framework may imply permanence. However, teaching frameworks evolve over time in relation to others, new learning, and experiences.

Acknowledging Our Apprenticeship of Observation

Even before beginning any official training, teachers are enculturated into the work of teaching while they are students. Sociologist Dan Lortie (2002) terms this process of enculturation "apprenticeship of observation." Through our years of apprenticeship in teaching as students, we encounter implicit frameworks about what it means to teach and learn ELA, including how teachers and students ought to behave and what they seek to accomplish in their classrooms. When we are students, Lortie notes, we evaluate teachers and their teaching, but we rarely, if ever, have occasion or reason to place teachers' actions within a pedagogical framework that offers a rationale for *why* teachers make certain decisions or take certain actions.

Early in our journeys to become teachers, it's not uncommon to think, "I'm done with the theory, let's get on with the real action." Like you, I recall itching to delve into the "real" work of teaching. Such thoughts, though, evidence the long-term effects of apprenticeship. Lortie (2002) uses the metaphor of a play to explain why the theory-action divide exists so prevalently. Students see "the teacher front stage and center like an audience viewing a play." Students, don't, however, "receive an invitation to watch the teacher's performance from the wings" where they might be able to access teachers' internal thinking or decision making, adjustments, reflections, autocorrections, and ongoing analysis of their own teaching (p. 62). Without this access, which really is beyond the purview of students, it makes complete sense that as students we focus on teachers' actions, rather than the framework that informs their actions.

In the shift from studenting to teaching, however, if we teachers do not develop and articulate framework understandings, we risk returning to the actions that appeared as tried and true recipes for successful teaching from our observations as students, especially when we encounter sticking points. The replication of these teaching strategies and actions without consideration for the frameworks they support can perpetuate persistent inequities in education.

One such dominant framework that pervades many students'—and, therefore, teachers'—apprenticeship of observation illustrates well the unintended consequences of uncritically adopting the actions of other teachers without considering the relationship between instructional choices and pedagogical frameworks. Brazilian educator Palo Freire (2018/1970) describes this dominant framework as *banking education*. Within this framework, students are viewed as empty vessels in need of filling from all-knowing teachers who deposit knowledge. Students, discouraged from questioning, are rewarded for their compliance and ability to regurgitate what the teacher deposits. Teachers dominate talk. Their goal is to maintain the existing system, which often privileges the already privileged. Although Freire wrote about banking education decades ago, there is, unfortunately, evidence that banking is alive and well in most of our experiences of apprenticeship.

Cruz's case offers such evidence. The administrator's questioning suggests her favoring of the banking framework. Cruz's mentor teacher, however, shifts the frame to focus the administrator's attention on the ways in which the noise reveals student engagement rather than uncontrolled chaos. Notably, both the administrator and mentor teacher share a commitment to student engagement. However, informed by divergent understandings about the kinds of learning made possible through student engagement, their frameworks suggest different pathways for achieving their shared goal. For the mentor teacher, student engagement results from meaningful social interaction and shared inquiry into pressing questions and problems. If student engagement looks to the administrator like quiet student listening, then we can assume that student engagement is the end product, the culmination of successful banking education where students are conditioned to value the teachers' expertise and knowledge.

Interactional Shift

Cruz's mentor's actions amplify a central understanding about how our frameworks and, by association, frames can and do shift in relation to other people and frameworks. The administrator shifted her understanding about what was going on in the classroom in relation to the frame the mentor offered. Ultimately, had his mentor teacher not shifted the administrator's frame because she shared framework alignment with Cruz, it's possible that Cruz would have felt pressure to assume the role of manager, even though it did not align with his framework commitments. For Cruz, shifting to manager would have meant becoming complicit in the perpetuation of inequitable classroom practices that privilege teacher over student voices, something he believes is central to the banking framework he actively works to resist.

We engage in and experience this process on a daily basis. Many of us, at least informally, study the frames people use and employ on social media platforms. We consider how they present themselves through what they say and what they don't say. In a meeting I attended recently, students expressed their frustration with people who only ever repost other people's postings. "I mean, don't they ever have anything to say themselves?" one student wondered aloud as others nodded.

The students' frustration was rooted in the fact that those who only ever repost never weigh in to ongoing or emerging discussions. Their expectation is that people interact with ideas in social media spaces by commenting or producing new content—to actively engage in framing and reframing the conversation. To them, an overreliance on reposting as the central mode of engagement on social media is akin to banking. Reposters keep recycling the status quo, rather than contributing new frames and, thus, contributing to the growth of new frameworks or framework understandings. In the minds of these students, at least, reposters have assumed a passive stance toward the social construction of knowledge and in doing so perpetuate unbalanced banking practices.

For these students, too, part of the frustration is that by not actively engaging in the framing of conversations, reposters seek to gloss or ignore their own positionality in the conversation. Who am I? What gives me a voice in the conversation? Why and how does my unique perspective matter? How is my perspective partial and situated in my own lived experiences? And, how might that recognition enable me to see the need for and advocate for others' situated experiences and insights, or ways of framing and contributing to the conversation?

Lived Experiences and Intersecting Identities

The students' questions highlight another important facet of how our teaching frameworks emerge and evolve. In addition to the frameworks that shape, often implicitly, our apprenticeship of observation and our interactions with others, frameworks for teaching and learning are shaped by our lived experiences and intersecting identities. Who we are, how we identify, how we wish to be seen by others, and who we wish to become all influence both how we interface with frames and, therefore, frameworks we encounter. This also influences the extent to which we seek to develop new framework understandings. This may especially affect those from historically marginalized and underrepresented populations in education as well as those who are aware of the ways in which they may have benefitted as majority students in inequitable schooling systems. For these teachers, the experience of schooling and apprenticeship as well as growing awareness of how their identities and lived experiences shape their involvement in schooling often motivate an eagerness to learn about, draw on, and develop new, more inclusive and just frameworks. As Jackie, a teacher candidate, reflects (see Box 2.2), recognizing these goals, though, also means remaining self-reflexive and aware of how our identities and experiences continue to position students in relation to us.

 2.2 Jackie, in her own words

Enacting socially just ELA instruction takes a lot of thinking and hard work. It means not just asking our students to go deeper but asking ourselves to think deeper as well.

Sometimes it can be challenging to surface our own assumptions and operational frameworks about teaching and learning as well as how they interface with our identities and lived experiences. Consider the possibilities in the reflective activity described in Box 2.3

☑ **2.3 Apply your understanding**

Because teaching frameworks are often implicit in our day-to-day lives, it can be challenging to begin exploring and identifying the frameworks that undergird your thinking about the work of ELA teaching and learning. One way to begin is to create a list of quotes that you feel best represents what you seek to accomplish or who you wish to become as an ELA teacher. While, of course, these quotes might come from texts specifically about ELA teaching or pedagogy, they may come from other sources as well, including but not limited to favorite literature or writing, speeches, spiritual or faith texts, elders, scholars, and philosophers.

List these quotes on a sheet or paper. Then, annotate these quotes. What do you find to be significant about this quote? What does this quote suggest to you about the work of ELA teaching and what it seeks to accomplish? How does the quote offer you a vision, or rationale, for who you wish to become as an ELA teacher?

Then, consider why these quotes matter a great deal to you as you contemplate them in relation to your identities and lived experiences. Annotate these quotes in this second layer of thinking. Perhaps you want to color code your annotations by choosing a different color to begin to make visible this layer of analysis and reflection.

If possible, share your quotes with a colleague. Invite that colleague to ask you further questions about why the quotes matter to you or stories about how the quote reflects well an approach to ELA teaching that is important to you. Afterward, record new insights that may have surfaced through the conversation.

Often, this activity begins to surface some of the key aspects of your evolving framework for ELA teaching and helps you put them into conversation with others' frameworks.

Choosing Frameworks

A variety of intersecting experiences inform which frameworks we choose to embrace and evolve. Assuming the role of teacher prompts reflection on our identities, experiences of schooling, and the frameworks that underpinned our apprenticeship of observations. At the same time, through our training, we encounter alternative frameworks for ELA teaching, which present opportunities to consider whether we pursue the pathways of our apprenticeship or new possibilities or both. This is especially true for we ELA teachers, because, as research has affirmed, our field includes a patchwork of frameworks that support and diverge from one another (Macaluso et al., 2016). Thus, the need to choose the frameworks we wish to pursue and for what purposes is an unavoidable part of becoming an ELA teacher.

 **2.4 Reflecting**

What kinds of instruction or pedagogy have dominated your experiences of schooling? How would you describe it?

Perhaps you experienced or witnessed teaching that does not seem congruent with socially just ELA instruction. How would you characterize that instruction? What is it about that instruction that you might choose not to follow or enact in your future teaching?

Not all experiences of schooling or apprenticeship of observation are inherently problematic or incongruent with socially just ELA instruction. It may be that you have experienced or witnessed teaching that you believe supports or embodies socially just ELA instruction. How would you describe this teaching? What is it about this instruction that you might choose to follow or enact in your future teaching?

With this choice comes a realization that no teaching framework is neutral. By definition, frameworks and the rationales they offer invite us to take a stance, a particular perspective, or point of view, about the work of ELA teaching and learning (Cochran-Smith, 1991). From a critical perspective, which views knowledge as socially constructed and "education [as] a political project embedded within a network of social institutions that reproduce inequality" (Sensoy & DiAngelo, 2017, p. 1), when teachers choose not to take action or claim neutrality, that, too, is a stance—at times, a stance in support of the status quo.

It follows then that ELA frameworks for teaching and learning are not equal. Some frameworks align more closely with the work of social justice.

A Pedagogical Framework for Socially Just ELA Instruction

The framework for negotiating sticking points that is the focus of this book aligns with pedagogical frameworks that seek to foster more just and equitable classroom cultures. In Figure 2.1, I share a pedagogical framework for socially just ELA instruction that is premised on a fundamental belief that if students and teachers live together in equitable classroom cultures, their ways of learning together make possible certain kinds of inclusive, relational work with others beyond classroom walls. Socially just ELA instruction, because it models for students how to use their literacy skills and understandings to contribute to just and equitable communities, offers students a vision of who they can become and what they can do when they, in turn, seek, foster, and contribute to similar communities beyond classroom walls.

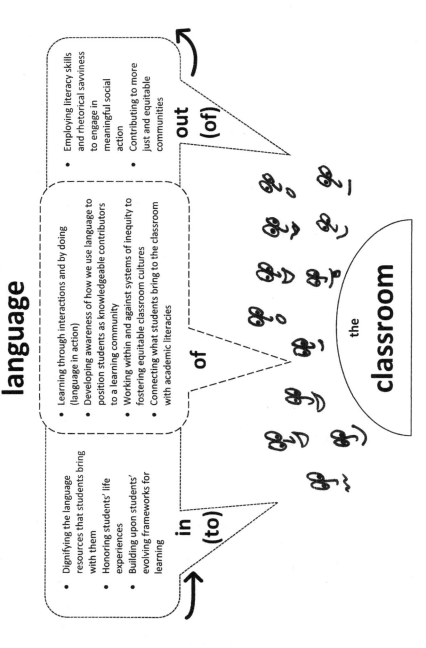

language

- Learning through interactions and by doing (language in action)
- Developing awareness of how we use language to position students as knowledgeable contributors to a learning community
- Working within and against systems of inequity to fostering equitable classroom cultures
- Connecting what students bring to the classroom with academic literacies

out (of)

- Employing literacy skills and rhetorical savviness to engage in meaningful social action
- Contributing to more just and equitable communities

in (to)

- Dignifying the language resources that students bring with them
- Honoring students' life experiences
- Building upon students' evolving frameworks for learning

of

the classroom

Figure 2.1 Socially just ELA framework for centering the language into, of, and out of the classroom

Key Concepts

To more fully explore the rationale for action that this framework promotes, consider the meaning of its key terms:

Socially Just

A focus on *socially just* emphasizes the social manner by which teachers, through their instruction, work to open opportunities for all students' learning. Embedded within this goal is a recognition that we can and should recognize and resist the reproduction of systemic inequities in our classrooms, schools, and communities. This emphasis aligns well with ELA instructors' commitment to teaching about how language (or, more broadly discourse, to include how people use verbal and nonverbal interactions) works in the world. *Socially just* encourages teachers to explore how we work within our classrooms for social justice as part of larger efforts to transform our society by removing the structures that create and perpetuate inequity. To achieve these aims, teachers distinguish between equality (where all students are treated equally, no matter the need) and equity (where students are given differential treatment, according to their needs). Teachers meld students' needs both for the language of dominant structures and practices with students' own knowledge, languages, and cultural literacy practices.

English Language Arts

Involving *English Language Arts* emphasizes the unique ways in which ELA teachers can utilize their disciplinary literacy skills and understandings to teach for justice. As a school content, ELA draws from many disciplinary traditions (e.g., literature, composition, rhetoric, creative writing, linguistics) which are united in their fundamental focus on the study of language to explore how people use their language for particular affects and action.

Instruction

Including *Instruction* in this framework focuses on pedagogy and, therefore, the full scope of ELA teachers' intellectual contributions to classroom life.

Of course, this work includes teaching, the act of facilitating learning live in-the-moment with students, but it also includes lesson, unit, and assessment design and reflection. It includes interactional choices that necessitate rhetorical savviness, as Ernest Morrell (2005) advocates, to effectively communicate and partner with families, administrators, colleagues, community members, and others with investment in our work. To partner in these ways enables us to raise awareness about the need to promote and enact educational changes that create more equitable systems of schooling and classroom learning. And a focus on instruction includes a fundamental assumption that effective instruction benefits from an inquiry stance toward on-going professional learning, the study of our teaching and students' learning, and efforts to continually adapt and adjust our teaching to what we observe and learn.

Taken together, then these three terms encompass the framework that underlies conversations about and efforts to enact socially just ELA instruction that are the focus of this book. Understood in relationship to one another, it's possible to see the wide range of ways in which teachers come to see and, in turn, enact socially just ELA instruction as more than teaching explicit content that is focused on social justice, as this exchange between three teacher candidates explores.

☞ **2.5 Morgan, Danny, and Lila, in their own words**

MORGAN: I've been realizing how socially just ELA instruction can be done in subtle ways. I think the way I executed the lesson was not outwardly socially just. The idea of literary theory has quite a bit of socially just nuances and meanings which created a socially just lesson. The lesson didn't necessarily teach social justice, but if the students grasp the deeper meaning of literary theory, then it sort of does. I enjoy this approach because the ultimate goal is for the students to make meaning of texts, including life, themselves rather than being told the meaning.

DANNY: Yeah. Totally. Acknowledging that socially just ELA lessons don't necessarily have to target a specific social issue but can also target processes and practices that allow students to analyze information and the world around them is an important thing not just because I feel like there is such a focus on covering specific issues, which is obviously important, but it's also important to help students pick up strategies to advance their position of reasoning to help them see why social justice work is especially important in their lives.

LILA: When I think about socially just instruction, I often only take into consideration the content that's being taught within a classroom. I've thought about the way things are taught in terms of teaching methods, but recently in my difficulty teaching with a colleague whose framework differed from mine, I'm beginning to think about the way things are presented or how we teach, the language we use. Teachers themselves are a critical part of socially just ELA instruction. It seems so obvious, but it's really much more complicated. You can't just have good intentions. You have to act on those intentions, and you have to do it with others.

Centering Language

This framework's attention to language emphasizes our role as teachers who consider the ways in which language plays a fundamental role in our efforts to foster more just and equitable learning cultures within our classrooms where we work and learn with others. Its attention to the language students bring into the classroom, the language that emerges through and becomes a product of classroom interactions, and the language that students take with them out of our classrooms that together highlight the ways in which teachers and students alike *use* language as much as we study language in ELA classrooms.

Figure 2.2 offers some examples of how teachers work to enact this pedagogical framework for socially just ELA instruction in their classrooms. It illustrates what it looks like when ELA teachers put this framework into action. The cases throughout the book offer similar practical examples of not only what it looks like but also what sticking points emerge as teachers work to enact their framework commitments.

A Working Framework

I offer this framework to clarify and ground the discussion of sticking points in the chapters that follow, but I do not wish to suggest that this framework is definitive, fixed, or unrelated to other frameworks. Quite the opposite, I want to make clear that this framework, like all teaching frameworks, and especially those that specifically speak to issues of social justice, is constantly emerging, shifting, evolving, and always in conversation with other teaching frameworks. This brings me back to our importance as teachers

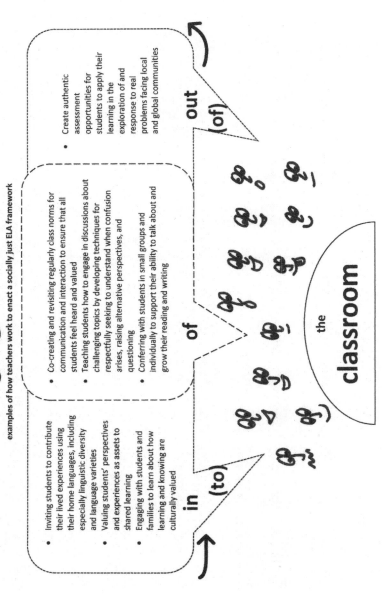

language in action

examples of how teachers work to enact a socially just ELA framework

- Inviting students to contribute their lived experiences using their home languages, including especially linguistic diversity and language varieties
- Valuing students' perspectives and experiences as assets to shared learning
- Engaging with students and families to learn about how learning and knowing are culturally valued

- Co-creating and revisiting regularly class norms for communication and interaction to ensure that all students feel heard and valued
- Teaching students how to engage in discussions about challenging topics by developing techniques for respectfully seeking to understand when confusion arises, raising alternative perspectives, and questioning
- Conferring with students in small groups and individually to support their ability to talk about and grow their reading and writing

- Create authentic assessment opportunities for students to apply their learning in the exploration of and response to real problems facing local and global communities

in (to)   of   out (of)

the classroom

Figure 2.2 Socially just ELA framework for centering language in action

who make critical decisions about which frameworks we adopt, adapt, and adjust as we journey forward. I make a central assumption that you share framework orientations for socially just ELA teaching, because you're reading this book. Your framework might include different language, elements, or emphasis. No matter, ultimately, it's up to you to decide how you articulate and evolve your framework for socially just ELA teaching in relation to others, including the mentors, students, colleagues, students, and scholars with whom you journey. What matters most is that you do so and that you continually revisit that framework as you encounter new frames and interactions in order to maintain clarity about where you're driving and why.

 **2.6 Reflecting**

No matter where you are on your journey to become the socially just ELA teacher you desire to become, reflecting on the evolution of your journey already can make visible how you've already begun to revisit and, perhaps, revise your framework understandings about what it means to teach ELA. To reflect on that progression, try mapping your journey from studenting to teaching. Create a visual representation or timeline of key events that you believe have shaped your framework understandings about what it means to teach ELA and teach for justice. These events or interactions might, of course, relate explicitly to your experiences of schooling (positive or not), but there might also be other life experiences that have shaped your reflections on the purposes and goals of your ELA teaching.

If possible, share your map with colleagues or a mentor. Invite them to ask you questions about what each event or interaction did to shape or reshape your framework for what it is that you seek to accomplish through your socially just ELA teaching. Take notes or record your conversation, as it may surface for you a deeper understanding or ability to articulate the evolution of your working framework in this moment.

Returning to this process across time may evidence important shifts in your framework commitments and understandings, which may help you reprioritize your instructional goals and decisions. Additionally, the process may also help you understand how others come to slightly different understandings, even if they share framework commitments. Those understandings may be equally important as you seek to work relationally with others.

Learning Cultures: The Contexts Where We Learn to Teach

Where We Put Frameworks into Action

At the start of the chapter, I shared my rocky journey through driver's education. It wasn't until I got out on the road that I began to understand the "real" work of driving. Similarly, we teachers are eager and enthusiastic about the "real" work of teaching in particular classrooms, schools, districts, and communities with particular students, colleagues, administrators, families, and community members. These places, or contexts, play an equally important role in the development and evolution of our pedagogical framework for socially just ELA instruction. Afterall, how we choose to enact our framework commitments should be intimately connected and responsive to the people, places, and cultures where we engage in the work of teaching. Many argue that our efforts to enact socially just ELA instruction should also seek to sustain and cultivate the contexts where we work and learn (Paris & Alim, 2017). To do that work, we carefully survey, study, and learn from the contexts where we teach, so that we can travel with care and intentionality.

Where We Straddle Insider/Outsider Positions

I spent six years of my childhood growing up in Germany. During that time, my mom taught me what it meant to be a hospitable cultural visitor. Among other things she taught me through her example, I learned the importance of not assuming that our German neighbors and friends ought to speak English or acclimate to our American cultural norms. Rather, I was expected to at the very least try out my German and study cultural norms, so that I could follow suit. "Our goal," she would remind me through words and action, "is for people not to see us as tourists." I was to humbly demonstrate my eagerness to honor cultural norms, acknowledging my uncertainty and asking for help or clarification when I bumbled the language or normative expectations. It wasn't always an easy process, but it was a rewarding one. I learned to check myself, my assumptions, and my perspectives as I grew aware of who I was in the context and how I could work interactionally within that context. In doing so, I grew not only in my awareness but also in my appreciation for all that I was learning and how that learning invited me into new ways of seeing people, places, and interactions. My efforts to acknowledge my outsider status while working to understand as much as I could about what it meant to be a cultural insider increased the likelihood that people would be willing to engage me, to share with and welcome me.

Journeying into a new classroom or school culture as a teacher is a lot like traveling to an unknown location, even when we may be familiar with that context from our experiences as a student. Or, maybe it would be more apt to say we do well when we travel into a new classroom or school culture not as tourists there to observe and take in the sights, but rather as those who humbly and excitedly seek to learn about and join the culture by acknowledging what we do not know, what we bring of ourselves and our learning, even apprenticeship, into the space, and, of course, how our evolving framework for socially just ELA instruction serves as a filter for what we see and seek in relationship with others.

☑ 2.7 Apply your understanding

As you prepare to go into a new school or classroom culture, consider that you may be traveling (metaphorically) to a new country. Just as it would seem unwise to randomly hop on a plane without researching to learn more about the cultural norms, customs, and languages of the people who live there, take steps to research what you can learn about the school before you arrive. The awareness you develop through your research can inform what you bring with you, what you hope to learn and experience, and how you seek to interact with others there. A move to research and learn more about a new school community can demonstrate an important deference to those who have more cultural knowledge and experience there than you. Taking such a stance and doing the thorough work of researching and preparing increases the likelihood that people will view you as someone who cares about building relationships by honoring those whose insider knowledge has much to teach you, and, thus, increases the chances that they'll be eager to work and learn with you, too.

If you know people with insider knowledge about the school, talk to them. Explore various online sources such as

- *The school's website:* What can you learn from the academic program or course guide, student handbook, social media feeds, announcements, biographies and writing from administrators, and/or department pages?
- *The school district's website:* What can you learn about the administrative leadership and their vision for the district, any major instructional or professional learning initiatives, and/or social media feeds? What do these sources message about what matters to the district?

- *Any state demographic information or report cards for the school or district:* What can you learn about the school's student and teaching population and demographics as well as academic performance (at least by the measures listed)?
- *Local community government, civic, or cultural pages:* What can you learn about the community in which your school is located, including its history, its future aspirations, economic drivers, cultural events or sites, social and community support networks or nonprofits, social and recreational events or opportunities for residents, and opportunities for student involvement and support beyond the school building?

As you review and read these sources, create a chart that captures your thinking and wonderings. What does this information suggest to you about what it means to be a student who attends this school? What seems valued or prized in the school or community culture? Of course, as you already can surmise, what you learn reflects and represents situated perspectives presented for public audiences. Who or what might be absent from the narratives or perspectives you're reading? Therefore, it will be helpful to log what you wonder based on what you've learned. What questions might you have that would help you understand more fully what it's like to be a teacher and student in this school context? Those questions might launch your inquiry as you engage in your earliest interactions with a mentor teacher, students, and other school community members.

What I notice	What I wonder	Source

Where Sticking Points Become Visible

What, then, is the relationship between the contexts where we enact our frameworks for socially just ELA instruction and sticking points?

Alex: Case Study, Revisited

In Chapter One, we met Alex whose choice reading assessment pathways left her with a sticking point: When given choice reading assessment options, only one student pursued the "advocacy option," which Alex considered to be most aligned with socially just ELA learning. We learned that in the department where Alex was working with her mentor teacher, choice reading was a staple of their pedagogical approach to ELA teaching. She, like the teachers in the department, was committed to helping students find pleasure in their choice reading. Her mentor often promoted his preferred choice reading in the mystery thriller genre, and that genre was well represented in his classroom library. Alex book talked texts that explicitly explored issues of injustice, inequity, and inequality as well as prioritized the lived experiences of historically marginalized peoples in diverse young adult literature. However, students gravitated toward their go-to genres and authors. While Alex found nothing wrong with their choices, she was aware that they were not selecting the texts or kinds of texts she was promoting. She believed in choice, but she noticed that students' assessment menu selections steered clear of the "advocacy option." Alex's sticking point emerged and became noticeable within the context of the classroom where she was working and learning to enact socially just ELA instruction.

Alex's case makes clear two interrelated foundational understandings about frameworks and the emergence of sticking points.

First, the contexts where we teach and learn, our classrooms, are crucible spaces whereby sticking points become visible. In other words, sticking points are contextually bound. What makes them a sticking point depends upon the specific dynamics and pedagogical framework for socially just ELA instruction at play in the particular contexts where we teach and learn.

Let's say many students in your class aren't completing their homework. Is that a sticking point, or not? Of course, it could be considered a general sticking point that many teachers navigate at least from time to time. But let's view it through the lens of our pedagogical framework for socially just ELA instruction. Is it a sticking point, or not? To determine an answer to that question, you'd have to consider what you know about your context. What do you know about students' lives outside of school? What do you know about how students view the role of homework in relation to their learning? How do you, your mentor teacher, or department frame the purpose of homework in conversations with students? And so on. To determine an answer to that question, you'd also need to filter it through your framework understandings. How, if at all, is homework completion an issue of equity? Do students physically have access to resources (e.g., technology, quiet space) to complete homework, if they desire? Do students have time to complete homework, if they desire? Or, for example, do their out-of-school obligations (e.g., jobs required for contributing to the economic stability of their families, responsibility for the care of siblings) preclude them from prioritizing homework, even if they desire? And so on. Only when we consider the particulars of our context and then our context in relation to our framework, can we distill whether something is a sticking point.

Where We Can Open Opportunities for Negotiation

Second, because our teaching occurs in dynamically shifting classroom contexts where concentrated interactions shape our instructional efforts, sticking points and, therefore, opportunities for negotiating them will inevitably occur.

There's a saying that teachers maintain their sanity when they close their doors to the chaos of the outside world—in school and beyond. The embedded assumption in that saying suggests that it is in fact possible to ignore everything else and control what happens within the space of our classrooms.

Of course, teaching within the physical space of our classrooms centers our attention on what happens there. The weight of our work rests in our everyday instructional decisions. These decisions create the charge, the catalyst for student learning. To be sure, then, as teachers we shape the classroom culture through our interactions.

However, in accepting that we shape classroom cultures, we must also accept the important corollary that others also shape our classroom culture. If teaching were all about us or what we could control, it would be a simple matter. But our teaching and students' learning within our classrooms are influenced by a set of overlapping interactions between and among students, mentors, colleagues, families, administrators, and community members. These people directly and indirectly influence what happens in our classrooms. Figure 2.3 offers a visual of this constant interactive dynamic. Each of the interactants (those people with whom we and our students interact) in Figure 2.3 in some way influence our classroom culture. And because these interactions are constantly shifting, their influence evolves and remains in dynamic motion.

As we think about these dynamics in relation to our negotiation of sticking points, acknowledging these realities can, at points, make us feel that we have limited control over how we respond. That's where our framework comes into play. It serves to ground our decision-making in the moment and across time. This is the most important part as we think about sticking points—*we can control how we react to these dynamics*.

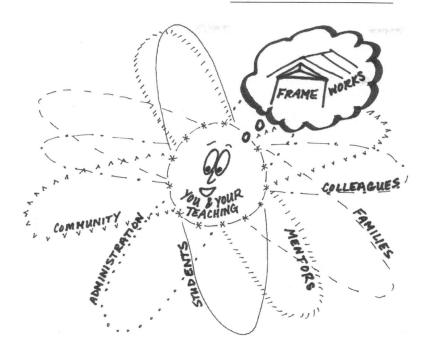

Figure 2.3 Interactional dynamics that influence teaching

Let's return to Alex's case for a moment to examine how sticking points can become welcome opportunities for redefining and strengthening our efforts to enact socially just ELA instruction in classroom contexts. For Alex, deciding how to react to her emergent sticking point was contingent upon her ability to read how it emerged in direct relationship to the context and interactions that shaped her instructional decisions. But it also emerged because she filtered these dynamics through her pedagogical framework for socially just ELA instruction. Without her framework understandings and commitments, she likely wouldn't have seen the fact that one student chose the "advocacy option" as a sticking point at all. It would have been a noticing, but not a sticking point. So, her context and her framework brought this particular sticking point into relief. It also provided her with an opportunity to pause and consider how she wished to proceed—how to negotiate the sticking point and take action.

What's noteworthy about Alex's reaction to the sticking point is that she approached it as an opportunity, a chance to reconsider her instructional priorities within her particular classroom and in relationship to evolving framework understandings about what it means to teach for justice. As teachers, we have a choice to see sticking points as roadblocks that prevent our progress from moving forward. We can try to control the interactional dynamics in our teaching lives. If we do, we risk not only burnout, we also risk abandoning our framework commitments. Yet, we can view sticking points as a natural part of our teaching lives. In this book, as you've already seen, I make an argument that the negotiation of sticking points can be an empowering and reenergizing aspect of our teaching lives and wellbeing. Viewed in an enterprising way, sticking points present us with opportunities to determine how we'll react, what we'll choose, and how those decisions can work to support and sustain our framework commitments to socially just ELA instruction across time.

References

Cochran-Smith, M. (1991). Learning to teach against the grain. *Harvard Educational Review, 61*(3), 279–308.

Freire, P. (2018/1970). *Pedagogy of the oppressed.* Bloomsbury.

Goffman, E. (1974). *Frame analysis: An essay on the organization of experience.* Northeastern University Press.

Lortie, D. C. (2002). *Schoolteacher: A sociological study* (2nd ed.). University of Chicago Press.

Macaluso, K., McKenzie, C., VanDerHeide, J., & Macaluso, M. (2016). Constructing English: Pre-service ELA teachers navigating an unwieldy discipline. *English Teaching: Practice & Critique, 15*(2), 174–189. doi: https://doi.org/10.1108/ETPC-02-2016-0035.

Moje, E. B. (2007). Developing socially just subject-matter instruction: A review of the literature on disciplinary literacy teaching. *Review of Research in Education, 31*, 1–44.

Morrell, E. (2005). Critical English education. *English Education, 37*(4), 312–321.

Paris, D., & Alim, H. S. (Eds.). (2017). *Culturally sustaining pedagogies: Teaching and learning for justice in a changing world.* Teachers College Press.

Scheff, T. J. (2006). *Goffman unbound! A new paradigm for social science.* Paradigm.

Sensoy, Ö, & DiAngelo, R. (2017). *Is everyone really equal?: An introduction to key concepts in social justice education* (2nd ed.). Teachers College Press.

Tannen, D. (Ed.) (1993). *Framing in discourse.* Oxford University Press.

Tannen, D. (1998). *The argument culture: Moving from debate to dialogue.* Random House.

Part II
Negotiating Sticking Points, An Interactive Process

In the Part II chapters, you will find the layers of an interactive process for negotiating sticking points in your field-based teaching experiences. By emphasizing how the process is interactive, we'll see how to identify and interpret sticking points to ultimately decide how we wish to respond. We'll also learn ways of shifting our interpretations and understandings of those sticking points based on what we learn as we spend more time in classroom cultures with learners and teachers who have a great deal to teach us.

In basketball, players' success is dependent upon their ability to embrace interactive processes. What exactly does that embrace look like? Basketball is, of course, a team sport, so individual players must develop the ability to assess and adjust their own actions in relation to others. To be successful, players constantly read teammates and opponents' actions and choices in-the-moment. These readings enable them to adjust their own play in response and in support of the team's shared goal: winning the game. As players work collectively toward that goal, they draw on and contribute to an overarching strategy, or framework, for playing the game against an opposing team. For players to contribute to a winning team strategy during the game,

DOI: 10.4324/9781003134442-4

they must employ a set of interrelated skills. Whereas during practice players may rehearse skills—often in isolation, during a game, they flexibly, fluidly, and quickly draw interchangeably on those skills as they respond to what's happening on the court and where the strategy suggests the team is headed.

The team's coach plays a unique role in this interactive process, too. The coach is responsible for establishing the strategy, or framework, for play against an opposing team. That strategy informs the practice plan in the days leading up to the game, and it also informs calls that the coach makes during the game. The coach, like the players, reads the game in-the-moment. She watches and assesses not only what her team is doing but also what the other team is doing. This reading informs the ways the coach advises players so that the team can responsively adjust their play. She offers feedback about how players are enacting the strategy and responding to adjustments live. And the process of interactive, responsive adjustment continues throughout the game in an iterative cycle.

It doesn't matter if you are no basketball aficionado; you still know this sort of interactive process well. Much in life depends upon our ability to responsively adjust as a part of this interactive process. Your experiences of studenting in school have been strengthened, no doubt, by your ability to engage this process. As a student you were a player, metaphorically speaking. Most of us were successful in school because we figured out how to read and adjust our performance in response to instructor's expectations—whether they were stated or implied. We learned how to play school.

In our socially just English language arts (ELA) instruction, we teachers, like coaches, are constantly engaged in an interactive process of reading and responding to sticking points in students' learning and, by association, our own teaching. Pre-service teachers are both players and coaches. You have a special vantage point in understanding the teaching-learning process from dual positions. This positioning affords you a unique opportunity to study and then engage fully in that process.

The chapters that follow introduce each layer of the process for negotiating sticking points: noticing, framing, inquiring, listening radically, naming, re-framing, and acting. For the sake of accessibility, I outline them in what appears a linear fashion in successive chapters. Keep in mind, though, that each layer of the process should be seen as recursive. That is, layers may prompt us to return to previous layers before proceeding or jumping ahead.

The recursivity of the process required for negotiating sticking points is a lot like the writing process. Often students assume, because of how they've been taught, that writing is a linear process. However, once we've lived as

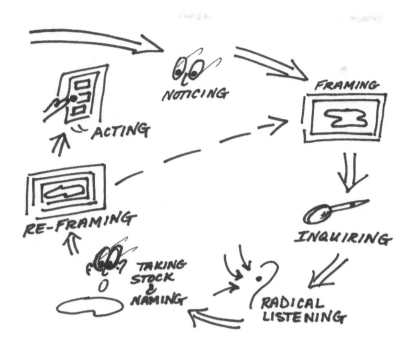

writers, we know well that writing is indeed a recursive, iterative process. For instance, we may be revising a paragraph or section of our writing and realize we need to go back to drafting as we see the need for greater clarity or possibility. But knowledge of the difference between generating ideas, drafting, researching, revising, editing, and publishing enable us to develop awareness of the utility and specific purpose of each step in this process so that we can take advantage of the fluidity and so that we don't lose heart when things get murky. We can trust that our ability to responsively adjust will benefit our writing and ultimately the message we convey to audiences.

Similarly, the process you'll learn in the following chapters will help you work fluidly and flexibly across and within layers to negotiate sticking points as they bubble up in your teaching and field-based interactions. Both beginning and veteran teachers I've worked with and learned from have, at times, shared in confidence, "I'm nervous. I know I don't know everything. How will I learn it all? What will I do if the unexpected happens?" The subtext of these questions surfaces another important truth about teaching: The unexpected will always arise. Sticking points will inevitably emerge. The confidence that comes from knowing and living the process you'll learn in Part II can reassure that there's a pathway forward for embracing the unexpected. There's no need to ignore sticking points. Instead, learning to responsively adjust your instruction using this interactive process can affirm that you'll be ready and prepared to read and respond carefully and thoughtfully to sticking points that emerge as you work to enact socially just ELA instruction. As a result, your negotiation of sticking points will help you strengthen your teaching and professional relationships.

3
Noticing: Identifying Dissonance

You'll recall that sticking points are spaces of dissonance between and among frameworks. Without the ability to notice dissonance or note the emergence of sticking points in our teaching, we miss opportunities to consider how we wish to act in response. Put another way, if we cannot notice framework dissonance, we risk compromising our ability to enact and strengthen our efforts to teach English language arts (ELA) for justice.

Circling the Roundabout

As the engineers of learning opportunities in our classrooms, we teachers face dissonance on a day-to-day basis. Our ability to notice such dissonance is a critical resource in our teaching lives. To understand how and why noticing dissonance can serve as a critical resource, let's consider an analogous example.

DOI: 10.4324/9781003134442-5

For years, civil engineers designed intersections around one of two basic building blocks: traffic lights and stop signs. These intersections worked well enough. Over time, though, a set of related factors have called into question the effectiveness of traffic lights and stop signs. Accidents at intersections have risen. Traffic volumes are increasing. Traffic patterns are changing. Vehicle type and weights vary more widely. Demands to save green space have gained public traction.

Noticing this dissonance has compelled civil engineers to revisit framework rationales for their design choices. They have asked, "What matters most, and how do we weigh shifting factors in relation to one another?" People's safety is, rightly, of paramount importance. Moving traffic most expediently through an intersection is key, too. But civil engineers are responsible to the cities and states who have hired them. So, cost must be a central consideration as well. Of equal importance are plans and visions for future growth and sustainability. These framework priorities offer civil engineers guidance in weighing which design choices enable them to serve the greatest good.

Reflecting on this dissonance in relation to framework commitments has led civil engineers to reconsider widespread reliance on traffic lights and stop signs. Citing evidence that roundabouts are a safer, more efficient, and less costly way to redirect traffic at intersecting roads, many civil engineers now embrace modern roundabouts (Dubner, 2021).

In our teaching lives, we, too, circle the roundabout of framework dissonance. Noticing—and ultimately negotiating—dissonance is directly connected to our ability to articulate and revisit the frameworks that inform our teaching. Put differently, if we don't have clarity about the frameworks that inform our instructional decisions, we won't see dissonance as an opportunity to pause in determining our next best action for the greatest good. Determining which action to take requires awareness, too, that there will always be multiple choices available to us and determining our next best action doesn't automatically mean that there are "right" answers. Rather, we can, like the engineers, make informed choices that result from weighing available options against our framework commitments.

Why Noticing Dissonance Matters

With all this in mind, avoiding dissonance may seem a preferred approach. Why notice and, by extension, seek to pursue dissonance when ignoring or sidestepping it seems like a smoother route, an easier and less stressful day-to-day? Choosing to do so, though, doesn't address the root problem. It often exacerbates it.

To clarify, let's revisit civil engineers' realization about roundabouts. As we'll explore more in future chapters, it is worth noting that the ways we choose to deal (or not) with dissonance, or sticking points, are consequential. Undoubtedly, roundabouts introduce confusion and stress for drivers who are unfamiliar with how to navigate them. It may seem at first that they introduce more upheaval than they are worth, except that people's lives are at stake. Short-term challenges, especially for people who are less familiar with civil engineer's framework-informed choices, do not outweigh the benefits to people's access and safety—the greater good—in the long run.

Acknowledging dissonance in our teaching lives reminds us that the everyday instructional decisions we make are hugely consequential. If we fail to notice dissonance, our students' learning lives are at stake. For those of us committed to socially just ELA instruction, failure to notice dissonance results in a missed opportunity to realize and strengthen our commitment to educational equity and justice. We risk acquiescing to other frameworks that may well be misaligned with our stated goals. We risk making and propagating decisions that threaten to perpetuate the very systems of inequity we seek to redress. Noticing dissonance is the first step in keeping our framework commitments at the heart of our decision-making.

Tools for Noticing Dissonance

Notetaking: Noticing "What's going on here?"

In the sections that follow, we'll explore tools for developing our capacity to notice dissonance in the classroom cultures where we're observing and interacting with students, mentors, and others. To begin our exploration, let's study an inductive puzzle. Figure 3.1 offers two field logs, which are notes that people take as they watch classroom instruction and interactions unfold live. They may be electronic or handwritten, as these notes originally were. Thus, they may be written in short hand and later returned to as observers seek to capture what happened live in-the-moment. These field logs represent two different observations of the same lesson which explains why you'll likely notice overlapping similarities. As you review both logs, consider where you notice the two align with and differ from one another.

Key
T – teacher
ST – student
"_" – direct speech

Field Log A		
Line Time	Speaker	Notetaking
1	T	Bell Objective [shows & reads from front screen] theme
2 :30	T	Connection to prior learning Develop understanding of theme & how it offers multiple perspectives on an issue
3 1:00	T	Relevance Links to social media & how people present a certain message about who they are through their postings Links to theme and process readers use
4 2:00	T	Direct instruction Explains link to earlier work with theme Shares: understand plot, identify key details, recognize stated relationships, make simple inferences, make complex inferences that require info from across text
	ST	Quiet and focused
5 5:00	T	Transition
6 5:30	T	Modeling Points to and reviews theme chart from previous class where ST brainstormed possible themes Picks one theme from chart Shares graphic organizer Does think aloud with excerpt from young adult literature text, decisions about what to include and why
	ST	Record T notes

Field Log B		
Line Time	Speaker	Notetaking
1	T	Objective Shows & reads from front screen: "I can identify how a theme in a text emerges for me as I read."
2 :30	T	Connection to prior learning Develop understanding of theme, "not moral, more complex," offers multiple perspectives on an issue
3 1:00	T	Relevance "Build on previous conversations about theme" Links to social media & how people present a certain message about who they are through their postings "What do they want me to understand about them from all these postings?" Links to theme and process readers use
4 2:00	T	Direct instruction "We're going to consider [shows slide] what readers must do to understand theme." Explains link to earlier efforts. Shares: understand plot, identify key details, recognize stated relationships, make simple inferences, make complex inferences that require info from across text
5 5:00	T	Transition
6 5:30	T	Modeling Points to and reviews theme chart from previous class where ST brainstormed possible themes Picks one theme from chart Shares graphic organizer Does think aloud with excerpt from young adult literature text, sharing thinking about how she's making decisions about what to include and why

Figure 3.1 Two field log notetaking examples from the same classroom observation *(Continued)*

7	T	Transition		7	T	Transition
10:00				10:00		

8	T	Guided practice		8	T	Guided practice
10:30		Class picks another theme from chart Sets up instruction Gives ST time to open the graphic organizer on their computers Tells ST to share thinking Shares predetermined groups on screen		10:30	ST T	"Practice this same process together" Sets up instruction: "work together to fill in the graphic organizer for this theme, just as you saw me model" Gives ST time to open the graphic organizer on their computers "Everyone should be ready to share group's thinking, if I call on you when we come back together" Shares predetermined groups on screen Suggests another theme from chart Other ST agree with suggestion and rationale provided

11	ST	Move into groups & begin work		11	ST	Move into groups & begin work
11:30		immediately All ST fill in their graphics organizers		11:30		immediately In groups, ST collaborate to complete graphic organizer, often interrupting to question "Why do you think that? How do we know that from what's here? Can we be sure?"

12	T	Circulating around the classroom,		12	T	Begins circulating around the
15:30		checking on groups' thinking, reading their graphic organizers as they talk Gives 2 min. warning		15:30		classroom "Talk me through this example here?" (pointing to a space on the graphic organizer) Affirms logic, but pushes for clarity: "What you just said is clearer than what's written here. Work to include those details you shared with me before we come back together." Another group: "I wonder what other evidence you can find for this claim. There's got to be more, don't you think?" Gives 2 min. warning

13	T	Calls class back together		13	T	"Ok, I think we're ready to come
20:30	 ST T	Calls individual ST to share out group thinking Adds ST thinking to graphic organizer on screen Asks ST to give examples to support their thinking		20:30	 ST	back together." Calls individual ST to share out group thinking Adds ST thinking to graphic organizer on screen Asks: "What textual evidence did you find to support your claim here?"

14	T	Transition		14	T	Transition
25:30				25:30		

Figure 3.1 *(Continued)*

15 26:00	T	Independent Practice/Conferring Gives directions
16 27:00	ST	Begin working quietly on their own in choice reading texts
17 29:00	T	Checks in with ST, looks at their graphic organizers Moves around the room to different ST Redirects some ST ST read in choice reading if done early
18 35:00	T	Wrap Up Repeats objective Shares feedback on what she's seen in their work
	ST	Links to next lesson: theme and poetry Submit their graphic organizers
19 38:00		Bell

15 26:00	T	Independent Practice/Conferring "Find section on graphic organizer for independent practice"
16 27:00	ST	Begin working, search through texts
17 29:00	T	Moves around the room to different ST, rather than waiting for hands and questions Whispers: "What theme have you chosen? Talk to me about how you came up with this claim. What evidence do you have to support that claim about the theme?"
18 35:00	T	Wrap Up Repeats objective "I noticed as I came around today that many of you were using explicit textual evidence and warrants to support your claims about themes in your texts." Links to next lesson: theme and poetry ST submit their graphic organizers
19 38:00		Bell

Figure 3.1 *(Continued)*

 3.1 Reflecting

After you've reviewed Figure 3.1, take time to reflect on what you noticed. What do the logs suggest about how each observer:

- approached the observational task?
- read the classroom instruction and learning?
- viewed the goals of instruction from their framework for ELA teaching?

What does each log foreground or background as you study each observer's noticings?

As you reviewed and reflected on the two field logs (Figure 3.1), you likely noticed how each log includes descriptive notes about what each observer sees. Both observers summarize the events that occurred in the lesson they watched.

An Ethnographic Approach to Noticing Classroom Interactions

Both observers take an ethnographic approach to noticing as they observe classroom interactions. Building on Carolyn Frank's (1999) book *Ethnographic Eyes: A Teacher's Guide to Classroom Observation* (1999), an ethnographic approach to classroom observations seeks to make visible "patterned and shared ways of interacting, understanding, and believing (Bloome, 1985)" in unique classroom cultures (p. 2). As Frank writes, this perspective encourages observers to position themselves as "learners, learning from members the cultural patterns" within the classroom they are observing (p. 3). With this goal in mind, when observers take an ethnographic approach, they prioritize "insider" perspectives and experiences—those of the mentors and students in the classrooms they are observing—rather than outsider perspectives, which can favor the observer's bias, even when that's not the intent. Through this prioritization of "insider" perspectives, observers come to recognize and see that there is more than one view of classroom reality. "In juxtaposing these views," Frank continues, "we come to see what is real from a variety of perspectives. To understand that there is never a completely objective account is to realize multiple perspectives" (p. 4). Ethnographic approaches to notetaking, because they surface multiple perspectives and frameworks, offer a tool for teachers like us to notice dissonance, or sticking points, in classroom observations and interactions.

Even with their shared ethnographic approach to observation, you likely noticed differences between Field Log A and B, too. You may have noticed how Field Log B includes more specific quotes that make more visible the language of the classroom, including the talk and interactions between and among the teacher and students. For example, in Field Log B, we see specific evidence in the form of direct quotes and interactional exchanges between the teacher and students in the guided practice and independent practice portions of the lesson (lines 8 and 12). As complete outsiders (those who did not have the opportunity to see this classroom and lesson live), the inclusion of these details offers us a better sense of how learning was constructed between and among members of the classroom. Even though they both adopt an ethnographic approach to notetaking, the inclusion of these details flags an important potential difference in what's visible through these field logs.

Our Socially Just ELA Instructional Framework Lens: Noticing Differently

The distinct details we see as we compare Field Log A and B (Figure 3.1) highlight that no observation is neutral. All noticing is necessarily filtered.

We have an observational agenda. That agenda is intimately connected to our framework commitments, which serve as a lens for answering, "What is it that I'm looking for or at?"

This realization is akin to processes and understandings that are quite familiar to us as ELA teachers. Consider for a moment the way our disciplinary training has prepared us to teach literature. As a result of our disciplinary content knowledge, we understand that critical lenses make possible new readings. As ELA teachers, we introduce students to various lenses readers use to analyze what they read. We show students how to apply critical lenses to their reading. And we help students understand how critical lenses make visible ideologies that might otherwise be invisible but at work in these texts and, by extension, our world (Appleman, 2015). Lenses help readers analyze how some ideologies offer insight into the propagation of racism, sexism, classism, linguicism, ableism, homophobia, xenophobia, and other intersecting injustices used to discriminate against people. Thus, critical lenses also offer readers tools for redressing these inequities.[1]

We take joy in helping students begin to put texts into conversation with one another, and celebrate the days when, because of our joint learning, they begin to see the value of choosing a lens to more closely examine questions that drive their inquiry, desire to rethink, and ability to create anew.

Similarly, our socially just instructional lens coupled with disciplinary knowledge position us uniquely well to home in on dissonance because it can flag opportunities to learn, explore, and strengthen our ability to create and contribute to classroom cultures that open opportunities for all learners. With this understanding in mind, reconsider Field Log B (Figure 3.1).

 3.2 Reflecting

As you reread Field Log B in Figure 3.1, this time consider how the observer's framework for socially just ELA instruction influences what the observer sees and highlights based on what they notice. Try highlighting or logging where you see evidence that the socially just ELA framework may prompt the observer to notice particular interactions, language, and actions over others. Use Figures 2.1 and 2.2 as a guide or prompt for carefully attending to how the framework filters the observer's noticings.

Then, if you can, talk with another reader or colleague about what they saw as they, too, studied Field Log B similarly. How might your conversation illuminate other things in your shared reading of that log?

Early in the lesson (line 3), the observer includes the specific ways that the teacher uses language to build relevance and connect the lesson to previous learning. More specifically, the teacher invites students to consider how authors make rhetorical choices to present themselves through their writing—in this case, social media postings. The teacher asks the class to consider how they read social media posts and, in doing so, authors, too. To capture this line of inquiry, the observer logs the question the teacher shares with the class: "'What do [authors] want me to understand about them from these postings?'" She's making clear that this is the question she has in mind as she reads social media posts.

The observer's efforts to log the teacher's language help to make visible the ways the teacher uses her questioning and explanations to achieve a series of overlapping socially just ELA instructional goals. She models for students her own thinking process so that they can gain access to the kinds of disciplinary thinking she'll ultimately ask them to try out in their own reading and writing practices. She builds relevance for students by connecting the work of the lesson to a literacy practice (critically reading social media), which students are well-accustomed to and already engaged in, even if they may not have fully realized. Moreover, she invites students to explicitly see and consider how authors—including the students in her classroom—actively shape and shift, if they choose, how they compose and, therefore, share their identities with audiences. In a few short line three comments, the teacher's language begins to open opportunities for future classroom conversation about (1) the way writers choose to or choose not to share certain aspects of their identities with particular audiences; (2) whether or not certain identities are privileged in certain rhetorical situations; and (3) how rhetorical situations and power structures influence who gets to say what when and who gets to be seen and viewed in the ways they choose or prefer. That the observer notes this language and these aspects of the lesson suggests that the observer is filtering their notetaking through a socially just ELA lens, which underscores the importance of opening conversations with students about how people use language to accomplish certain goals and enact identities as well as how systems of oppression continue to foreclose opportunities for some marginalized identities and voices to accomplish their goals. These are matters of equity and inclusion, justice and injustice.

Examples such as the one in line three suggest that, in the eyes of the observer, the teacher is successfully enacting socially just ELA instruction. But what about dissonance? Where, if at all, in the observer's notetaking do we see an awareness of dissonance? This may be less visible to us.

Let's dig deeper and see where there might be evidence of how the observer's notetaking surfaces potential dissonance. First, remember from Part I that sticking points can emerge in a host of different ways. Of course, it's most easy to see dissonance when two people are talking about differences of understanding, rationale, or decision-making. However, there are other possibilities, too. We know that sticking points don't always surface as visible conflict between two people's frameworks. It's not uncommon for sticking points to become evident to us and not to others. So, for example, sticking points, and therefore, dissonance, may emerge in our observations as we consider the actions that another person, often a teacher, takes which may not appear to align with our framework rationales for action. But sticking points can also emerge in student responses. So, for example, we might be expecting certain kinds of student uptake in understanding or rehearsing a lesson objective or skill. As we teach a lesson, however, students may become confused or take up the lesson objective in ways we hadn't imagined or planned, ways that might not align with our framework vision.

There's an example of this very sort of everyday dissonance in Field Log B when we look more closely at line 11. As students are working on a graphic organizer, the observer notes that in some groups students ask one another, "'Why do you think that? How do we know that from what's there? Can we be sure?'" Then, as the teacher "begins circulating around the classroom," (line 12), she asks students to "'talk me through this example here.'" One of the first things I notice about these notes in Log B is how the observer saw more than just students filling in the worksheet or assignment. That the observer notes student questioning of one another and the teacher's questions about the expectations of the task suggests that there may be some dissonance in students' ability to evidence their understanding of theme as they worked to log their thinking on the graphic organizer. In the inclusion of these details, I'm struck by how the notetaking surfaces a place where perhaps what the observer saw and expected to see as students set to work was different from what happened as the lesson proceeded. These spaces of incongruence as we apply our framework understanding to classroom observations can help to surface dissonance, and by extension, sticking points. Here some of the students' peers and their teacher appear confused about whether students fully grasp what's being asked of them.

It is in the observer's efforts to include specific language by way of direct quotes that we can see (1) this dissonance at work in the classroom interactions; and (2) how the teacher is working to gain an understanding of student learning and progress through her questioning. The teacher is definitively not concluding, it seems to me from what the observer has noted, that the students are or are not fully grasping the lesson objective. Rather, we see the teacher work to understand the nature of the emergent sticking point. She uses her language to seek clarity about the dissonance, or sticking point, that's emerging through her own observations, careful listening to student interactions, and then student responses to her solicitation of their thinking and metacognition. The observer's efforts to home in on classroom language help us see where and why the dissonance emerges not just for the observer but also, presumably, for the teacher, given her efforts to gain further information and insight from students.

Seeing Everyday Sticking Points

These short exchanges in Log B may initially have seemed so commonplace that they didn't strike you as a space of dissonance, a sticking point, embedded in the lesson. Yet, in addition to more visible sticking points (e.g., when a student offers a racist interpretation of a text or when a guardian questions a text you've chosen on the grounds that its content is too controversial), if we are committed to enacting socially just ELA, every day sticking points such as this one are equally important for us to notice. Everyday sticking points become the backbone of our teaching lives. What's more, they can serve as valuable resources that, when we pause to notice and in so doing surface them, can help us unlock possibilities for more responsively adjusting our instruction in order to open opportunities for all students' learning.

In the case of Field Log B, the observer sees through their notetaking an everyday sticking point of this very kind. We have the added bonus of seeing how the teacher works to negotiate the sticking point live, too. She doesn't prematurely jump to a conclusion about students' ability to enact the objective. Rather, she seeks greater understanding of student thinking so that she can formatively assess their ability to enact the objective. This solicitation of student thinking yields important clarity for the teacher. As she listens, the teacher realizes that students are on the right track in their thinking. Their challenge is in the ability to log that thinking on paper. This realization allows her to offer targeted feedback to students, so that they can adjust and strengthen their efforts immediately. We see evidence of this when the observer notes the teacher's response to one group's thinking aloud: "'What you just said is clearer than what's written here. Work to include those details you shared with me before we come back together'" (line 12). The teacher is affirming that students have a solid understanding of the lesson objective.

However, they haven't fully captured that understanding in their written responses on the graphic organizer. Had the teacher chosen not to solicit student talk that enabled them to orally evidence their understanding, she may have concluded that they weren't fully able to enact the lesson objective. The observer's inclusion of specific language—both student and teacher language of the classroom—as well as specific instructional choices makes visible for us as readers the ways in which this teacher was working to formatively assess and adjust instruction live in the moment in response to student interactions.

In turn, we see in this example how our own notetaking can illuminate spaces of dissonance that align with our framework understandings. Developing tools for honing our ability to notice everyday sticking points offers us space to grow in our ability to, like this teacher, strategize and respond strategically without compromising our commitment to socially just ELA instruction.

Combining an Ethnographic Method and a Socially Just Lens

What, you may be wondering, then, is the relationship between an ethnographic approach to observation and a framework in our ability to notice dissonance? To be clear, it's not that we adopt either an ethnographic stance *or* the socially just ELA instructional framework as we observe and interact with students, mentors, and others in field-based classrooms. Our framework offers us a lens for filtering what it is we're looking at and for as we observe, and an ethnographic approach offers us a method for documenting our observations.

You may be surprised to learn that the observer in Field Log A and B is the same person. Gabriel recorded both logs. The first, Log A, he recorded live as he watched the lesson transpire. Luckily, for the purposes of revisiting the lesson, Gabriel's mentor teacher was recording her teaching to model with and for Gabriel how important it is to revisit one's teaching, to slow it down in order to consider again what can be seen and understood by carefully attending to what occurred and what was said. After Gabriel learned about the distinction between ethnographic fieldnotetaking and filtering one's notetaking through the framework of socially just ELA instruction, he returned to the digital recording of the lesson. As he rewatched the lesson, he used his Field Log B notetaking as a space to consider the relationship between ethnographic notetaking and a socially just ELA instructional lens.

In the Field Log B exchange in lines 12 and 13, for example, Gabriel chose to record direct language. This choice reflects Gabriel's adept use of ethnographic notetaking to capture what was occurring in the classroom.

Ethnographic notetaking illuminates *how* the observer makes notes. However, there were likely hundreds of other language moves that both the students and his mentor teacher made during this particular lesson. Gabriel carefully selected and highlighted some language and actions over others. These choices about what to highlight and record were informed by Gabriel's framework lens.

Our lens illuminates *why* we notice *what* we do. An ethnographic approach offers us a way of applying our socially just ELA instructional framework to classroom observation and interaction. Used in combination, this method and lens invite us to take a particular kind of position as we seek to view classrooms from the perspective of insiders while considering how the happenings, the instruction and learning in the classroom, serve to support equitable teaching and learning that open opportunities for all learners. They are mutually supportive in our ability to notice dissonance.

With the clarity of our socially just ELA instructional framework in mind as we assume an ethnographic stance toward observation, we begin to notice differently. As Figure 3.2 clarifies, in our notetaking, for example, we document the language of the classroom, watch how it offers us evidence of how learning occurs in the classroom, and begin looking for whose language(s) is (are) privileged. Our noticings are premised on framework understandings that student language and experience is a critical resource for supporting

Ethnographic approach	**Our goal** Descriptive observations that summarize what happened **What we notice** • What's happening from a nonjudgmental perspective? • How do class activities and events occur? Who is doing what? What is being said?
+ Socially just ELA framework lens	**Our goal** Observations of classroom talk and action as evidence to support description of how teachers and students interact during the lesson **What we notice** • What do I see happening from the perspective of the members of the classroom culture (insiders)? • How are classroom activities and events constructed between and among members of this classroom culture? • Who is doing the speaking when? And who is not speaking? **How to focus our noticings** • Where do insiders seem to do things or say things that seem incongruent with your expectations or understandings about ELA learning or teaching in this context? Or classrooms more generally? Describe these moments in as much detail as possible.

Figure 3.2 Notetaking

learning and, therefore, engagement in classroom culture. We also become more attuned to how teachers use language to support learners and learning. In short, our socially just ELA instructional framework invites us to notice through the lens of justice and equity. And, because we're concerned with issues of equity and inclusion, we're especially mindful of spaces and inter-actions where students can access learning that matters in their lives, of the extent to which students can bring their identities as assets to classroom learning, or we can foster students' sense that their literacies can be used to positively influence social change.

☑ **3.3 Apply your understanding**

With the benefit of Gabriel's example field logs (see Figure 3.1), either

- Revisit a set of field notes that you may have previously taken. Notice whether or how you were taking an ethnographic approach and applying a socially just ELA framework lens.
- Or practice field notetaking live in a classroom where you are currently observing and interacting. You might notetake as you watch your men-tor or a colleague teach. Or try recording your own teaching and return to it to take field notes ethnographically and through the socially just ELA framework lens.

Then, annotate your notetaking to surface for yourself (and maybe oth-ers, if you're lucky enough to be able to talk with others about it) how you're using an ethnographic approach to notice through a socially just ELA instructional framework lens. What do you see or focus on with the benefit of that lens?

✍ **3.4 Reflecting**

After you've completed box 3.3, reflect in writing or with others on what you noticed in your field notetaking and annotations. How is the process helping you begin to surface dissonance? Or is it? What do you need or want to continue to practice? To see? To understand about the process and what it makes visible?

Serene: Case Study

To explore further how teachers use a framework for socially just ELA instruction as a lens for noticing dissonance, let's focus on Serene's field experience. On this day, as Serene moved around her mentor teacher's classroom, she pulled up alongside a small group of students who were working on an assignment. Later, in a conversation with colleagues, she shared how dissonance quickly emerged when she encountered a student whose comment posed a sticking point:

☞ **3.5 Serene, in her own words**

One of the students in the group I worked with, Kurt, told me that he was not able to fully comprehend the book he was reading.

"They are only words on a page," he said.

I wasn't sure what to do, but I wanted to understand better whether or where he was really struggling. I didn't know him well, so I wasn't sure how to read his comment. Could he read? Could he not read? Could he read but not understand? I wasn't sure. So, I asked him to read to me. At first, he held back a bit and said he was not able to, but then eventually he did read a passage to me.

Although Serene wasn't entirely sure how to proceed initially, she noticed the dissonance. She saw Kurt's comment as a potential sticking point, because her socially just ELA framework revealed the need to understand what prompted Kurt's comment. She continued.

☞ **3.6 Serene, in her own words**

For me, the challenge was in understanding what Kurt did and did not understand about the text. I needed to understand how he was making meaning of the main points in the text to assess how best to help him. From a socially just ELA framework, I wanted to be sure to demonstrate critical caring for him as a learner in my classroom, and I wanted him to feel safe sharing his difficulties. At the same time, I wanted to be able to assess the root of his struggles to consider how to help him. I thought about how he may have come up through a system of schooling that may have missed the fact that he was a dependent reader and that the text we were reading was causing him difficulty. I thought, too, though, honestly, about whether he was struggling or whether he just didn't want to read to me or engage in the work assigned. I needed to figure out what was really going on so that I could figure out what to do. But I also worry that asking him to read aloud may have made him feel more put on the spot if he was finding the passage challenging to read, even on a literal decoding level.

Serene's sticking point prompted her decision to ask Kurt to read aloud, even though she wasn't sure what she would learn or even if it was the right decision. And to be sure, that hesitancy was an asset in her ability to notice and seek clarity about the nature of the sticking point. Her framework understandings affirmed the need to assess whether Kurt's response reflected his dependency as a reader or something else. This move to learn more from and about Kurt, about the nature of the sticking point, also suggests that Serene was aware that she may need to rethink and resee the dissonance in light of what she learned.

☞ 3.7 Serene, in her own words

I responded to this sticking point by allowing Kurt to read a small portion of dialogue that he could, I thought, read easily on his own. He was able to explain the idea in the text and expand on it, too. They weren't really just words on a page for him. The next conversation that we had together was related to the questions about conflict that my mentor teacher had posted on the board. He was able to quickly answer them with an explanation that showed his understanding.

By asking Kurt to read and talk about his reading, Serene determined that he was able to comprehend the text and address the questions about conflict.

Guided by a framework for socially just ELA, Serene understood well that her observations played an important role in her ability to notice dissonance. While this affirmed for Serene that Kurt could be successful in completing the assignment, she still couldn't be sure what had prompted Kurt to say, "They are only words on a page." She had more questions, which drove her desire to learn more about what motivated Kurt and his classroom interactions as she continued to observe and participate in the classroom.

Serene's case highlights the importance of strengthening our ability to apply our socially just ELA framework understandings in order to notice dissonance at work in classrooms and our teaching practice. It's a case that affirms how the ability to notice sticking points in our classroom interactions benefits from careful ethnographic notetaking—whether on paper as in the field logs in this chapter or orally as here in Serene's sharing with colleagues.

As the engineers of learning in our current and future classrooms, our ability to enact socially just ELA instruction is predicated on a closely related ability to notice dissonance. Like the civil engineers who began to see dissonance in assumptions that because stop lights and stop signs work well in some cases and places, they will continue to serve the good of all forever, our careful ethnographic notetaking allows us to notice dissonance and actively work against assumptions that the status quo equitably and justly serves all students well. These noticing prompt us to begin interpreting what we've seen, heard, and participated in as we engage in the work of the field. This move to begin interpreting is where we'll turn our attention next.

☑ **3.8 Apply your understanding**

As you become more involved in the work of teaching, it may seem difficult to maintain or develop your notetaking skills. We can learn a lot from veteran teachers who see notetaking as central to negotiating everyday sticking points that are a normal part of teaching for those committed to socially just ELA instruction. As you become more adept at notetaking, consider how your notetaking can occur even during your teaching of a lesson:

- Keep a notebook handy for quick notetaking; or
- Carry a pad of sticky notes with you while you teach, so that you can take short notes.

Then, between classes or as soon as possible, return to those notes to build on them with context details and observations.

Note

1 For extended conversation and instructional support for thinking about critical theory lenses and how they support socially just ELA instruction see Appleman

(2015), Ramirez and Donovan (2021), Ribay (2019), and Sarigianides, Petrone, and Lewis (2017).

References

Appleman, D. (2015). *Critical encounters in secondary English: Teaching literary theory to adolescents* (3rd ed.). Teachers College Press

Dubner, S. J. (Host). (2021, 10 March). Should traffic lights be abolished (No. 454) [Audio podcast episode]. In *Freakonomics*. M. Diduch. https://freakonomics.com/podcast/roundabouts/

Frank, C. (1999). *Ethographic eyes: A teacher's guide to classroom observation.* Heinemann.

Ramirez, E., & Donovan, S. (2021). Harm and healing: Reading with an ABAR (anti-bias, antiracist) lens. *Voices from the Middle, 28*(4), 54–59

Ribay, R. (2019). Critical theory as preparation for the world (2019 ALAN Workshop speech). https://randyribay.wordpress.com/2019/11/26/critical-lit-theory-as-preparation-for-the-world-2019-alan-workshop-speech/

Sarigianides, S. T., Petrone, R., & Lewis, M. A. (2017). *Rethinking the 'adolescent' in adolescent literacy.* National Council of Teachers of English.

4
Framing: Interpreting What You're Seeing

In Chapter Three, we explored the value of observational notetaking as a tool for noticing dissonant spaces or interactions where something seems misaligned with our framework understandings and goals. Without the ability to notice dissonance, we miss opportunities to support learning that is aligned with our commitment to socially just English language arts (ELA) instruction.

DOI: 10.4324/9781003134442-6

Framing Defined

Of course, we can't observe and notice forever. As teachers, we must ultimately respond. In our journey to respond, we interpret what it is that we're seeing. Often, we interpret based on our background experiences and knowledge, but we also interpret in relation to our ongoing learning and interactions in and about schools, teaching, and learning, which may differ from our background experiences and knowledge. The act of interpreting the sticking point is called **framing**.

Even for as much as we are noticing others' perspectives with the benefit of careful notetaking, a sticking point may emerge for us and not necessarily for others. Thus, we actively work to describe—at least temporarily for ourselves—what constitutes each sticking point. Framing helps us portray the essence of sticking points by answering, "How can I capture what's going on here?" Ultimately, as we'll see, framing helps us more easily hold onto a sticking point long enough to consider and make decisions about how to respond.

Of course, as ELA teachers, you're aware that framing, the verb, is different from frame, the noun. This distinction is important in understanding more fully what framing is and what it offers us. If you think of a frame on a picture or the way a camera lens serves as a frame for a photograph you might take, this noun form focuses on a constant, fixed demarking and limiting of a view. The frame marks what is included in the image. It serves as a boundary object that focuses our cognitive attention. The verb form of framing is still about focusing our attention, but it is much less about fixed and static boundaries. Rather, it is about the process we undertake to catalogue, even for the time being for ourselves, how we understand "what's going on here." Framing serves to focus our interactional attention.

Why Framing Matters

Framing allows us to describe the nature of the sticking point with full awareness that our understanding of and decisions about a sticking point will likely shift as we learn, observe, and interact more in the classroom(s) where we're living.

If this talk of framing feels a bit abstract, rest assured, you actively frame sticking points in your life beyond classroom spaces all the time. You use your noticings and background knowledge to interpret interactions thousands of times each day. Often, we frame interactions automatically and without full awareness that we're doing so. But we become more fully aware of our efforts to frame interactions when we notice dissonance between or within frameworks. How many of us, for example, have at some point thought we really knew and felt close to a person only to have that person act in a way that posed a real sticking point? The person's interactive choices may have caused us to question whether that person was really as close to us as we had believed. Their actions seemed misaligned or incongruent with your framework for how a best friend, love, or close relative should behave or for what they should say. Their actions posed a sticking point and caused you to consider how best to frame the relationship. You might ultimately have chosen to reframe the relationship. We'll return to reframing in a future chapter. For now, though, the point is that we frame and carefully consider our framing of relationships, interactions, and situations all the time. The ways we work to frame things help us hold on to abstract understandings about those relationships, interactions, and situations.

Tools for Framing Sticking Points

Notemaking: Interpreting "What's going on here?"

Building on notetaking, notemaking goes beyond noticing to begin interpreting, or framing, the sticking points that emerge as we observe and engage in classroom cultures. Figure 4.1 summarizes the notemaking step in our process of negotiating sticking points.

Acknowledging Our Situated Perspective

As we confirmed in Chapter Three, our noticing is always filtered. Thus, our interpretations of what we're noticing are always filtered, too. Who we are and what we've experienced necessarily position us in particular ways to interpret the sticking points we see. We bring to the interpretive table unique vantage points that predispose us to see and understand sticking points differently from others whose identities, lived experiences, and learning are distinct from our own. That unique positioning can serve us well at times, but it can also act as a hindrance to our interpretations of sticking points, too.

How, then, do we develop awareness of how unique positionality influences our interpretations? Together, an ethnographic approach and a socially just

Ethnographic approach	**Our goal** Interpretations of, assumptions about observations **How we begin interpreting what you're noticing** • What am I seeing from my perspective? • What meaning of this event, interaction, language, action do I make?

+ Socially just ELA framework lens	**Our goal**
	Interpretations of, assumptions about observations from my situated perspective, cultural biases
	How we continue interpreting what you're noticing
	• What am I seeing from my situated perspective, as I seek to recognize and acknowledge how my cultural biases are necessarily filtering what I see and look for? How might the following language prompts help me make visible my situated interpretations?
	  o "I'm not used to seeing . . ."
	  o "I think . . ."
	  o "I'm noticing . . ."
	  o "It seems to me that . . ."
	• Which classroom interactions (talk and actions) open or foreclose opportunities for student learning?
	• Whose voices are prioritized and privileged?
	• How is power circulated in this classroom culture?
	• How do teachers and students orient toward one another? How are they positioned in relation to one another?
	• What sticking points emerge for me as I observe from my situated perspective?
	• Why does this dissonance seem to matter to me? What seems significant about noticing this sticking point?

Figure 4.1 Notemaking

ELA framework work in concert to help us carefully consider our interpretative positionality. They help us ask and, later, make visible for others, "Who am I to be interpreting what I'm observing and noticing?" Our framework encourages us to connect our framing to our situated perspective, which requires also acknowledging that our perspective is inherently culturally biased. Often, we see or are encouraged to see biases as negative, which can encourage us, at times, to keep them hidden. But, working together, an ethnographic approach provides us a means by which to log our framing and surface the ways in which our interpretations of classroom observations and interactions are necessarily situated in our lived experience. Surfacing our situatedness, the position from which we interpret, can become a real asset not only in strengthening our ability to interpret but also in our ability to invite others into our interpretations and understandings about particular classroom cultures. In other words, acknowledging and naming our cultural perspectives and inherent biases can help us acknowledge first for ourselves and then for others the basis from which we are making interpretations about sticking points. If we can connect the dots between our own vantagepoints and our interpretations, we help others see the interpretative tissue that connects our framing.

Approaching notemaking in this way is analogous to how we might invite students to consider the moves they make when developing a written argument. Early on without the benefit of instruction, students often kerplunk a piece of evidence and a claim on a page. They often assume readers will do the connective work needed to tie evidence to a claim. Without instruction about how to tie evidence to a claim with warrants, writers miss an opportunity to help readers see how they are building the relationship between evidence and claim. Warranting offers the means by which writers take readers with them in tracking the logic of an argument within and across claims. It also creates space for readers to ultimately weigh in, too. Readers can join writers in affirming or questioning the viability of their arguments.

Tied to notemaking, acknowledging our situated perspective as a part of the framing process is the key to remaining cognizant of how our interpretations are partial and derived from experience and situated perspectives. This acknowledgment enables us to remain open to and welcoming of others' interpretations of similar and related sticking points. Framing that includes acknowledgment of our situated perspectives and cultural biases can create space for colleagues and mentors to join us in affirming or questioning the viability of our interpretations, even if or maybe especially because they don't necessarily share our perspectives, biases, or experiences.

I'm reminded of a moment where my awareness or lack thereof of my own situated perspective became clear to me. I accepted my first teaching job in a rural, small-town community. It was, in fact, the smallest town I had ever lived in. As the fall semester proceeded, I learned that students were given a day off from school to go deer hunting. There was excitement in the halls and banter between students about where they would be hunting based on their earliest scouting efforts and access to family, friend's, or public land for hunting. My colleagues told me that if school weren't closed at the opening of the hunting season, there would be too few students in attendance for the school to be able to qualify that day on the academic calendar by state regulations. During homecoming week, one of the dress up days was even "hunting day," and most students would wear their camouflage to school in celebration of a shared recreational passion. It was clear: Deer hunting was a big deal.

Before the big day, I overheard yet another group of students talking about past hunting seasons and the deer they were able "to bag." One student gloated, "Well, I got that fifty-point buck with my grandpa last year." And another poked, "Yeah, right. The best you've gotten is a seven pointer."

In my earnestness to acknowledge confusion and learn more about a culture to which I was a complete outsider, I asked, "Who awards the points?" The classroom erupted in laughter.

Clearly, the joke was on me, but I had no idea how or why I had misspoken. I sheepishly smiled and let them laugh on for a bit as I reflected on my prior conclusions. I had seen these small stands and stadium canopies at area gas stations where hunters registered the deer they shot with the state's Department of Natural Resources. I assumed some specially trained official therein awarded hunters points and prizes. That must have been part of the sport and ability to earn bragging rights, I concluded.

When the laughter finally settled, one glad student happily educated this new, clueless teacher. "Okay. Points are the number of tips on a buck. The older the buck, the more points. And you count them once you've bagged [shot] your buck to see how big its rack [antlers] is. There's a whole system you learn you know when you're young. No one's out there counting for you or awarding you points." Everyone, including me, laughed again at this major cultural misunderstanding.

I had applied my understanding of points and prizes, not unlike cultural norms in many school settings, to deer hunting. The misalignment struck my students as hilarious. I had clearly flagged myself as a cultural outsider. Years later, they'd stop by my classroom or see me in town and laugh about this misunderstanding. But what this episode also makes clear is the importance of checking our assumptions and situated understandings. I was applying a framework for points to this discussion that was misaligned with students' frameworks about points in the context of this conversation. Acknowledging my limited cultural understanding in the end helped students see the need to clarify and me to learn from their insider knowledge. The context here mattered deeply as did my ability to check my understandings before proceeding.

Because of our deep commitment to socially just ELA instruction and wish for our interpretations of sticking points to ultimately help us understand and seek to create classroom cultures that open learning opportunities for all students, being able to track our own and invite others into our framing of sticking points enables us to gain greater clarity about the nature of what we're seeing. As a result, we can act with confidence that our interpretations (notemaking) are viable and grounded in evidence (notetaking) as well as aligned with our socially just ELA instructional framework.

To make clearer what our framing makes visible for us, let's return to Gabriel's field logs from Chapter Three. In Figure 4.2, you'll see how Gabriel differently approached the work of notemaking in his efforts.

Field Log A			Field Log B		
Line Time	Speaker	Notemaking	Line Time	Speaker	Notemaking
1	T	• ST focused and eager to learn • T sets purpose for the lesson • No wasted time getting into the lesson	1	T	• T uses "I can" statement objectives/learning targets to position ST as knowledgeable, capable readers and doers • Makes transparent the shared learning goal
2 :30	T		2 :30	T	• T tries to clarify a common misconception about theme, which could pose a challenge for readers
3 1:00	T	• ST see connection to "real world" outside of classroom • T builds engagement	3 1:00	T	• Emphasizes the social construction of meaning making in texts of all kinds and relates that meaning making to social media and STs' expertise in navigating those spaces as adept readers • Poses genuine, authentic inquiry questions that drive class learning together
4 2:00	T	• Establishes clear link between direct instruction and modeling	4 2:00	T	• Equip ST with understandings necessary to engage fully in the inquiry-driven learning task for the lesson . . . provides ST with the tools to do the inquiry work
5 5:00	T	• Transition	5 5:00	T	• I'm not used to seeing such a clear lesson logic, which makes it easy for ST to see a clear focus for shared learning.
6 5:30	T	• Links well to previous learing with the chart • ST track T thinking on their graphic organizer notes, so they have a model to return to	6 5:30	T	• Offers a think aloud to make visible the thinking process that the T wants to invite ST to try out and on in the work of the lesson • The modeling does not focus on what to think as much as how to develop an understanding of how themes emerge for us as we read a text, rather than as something we search for or a "lesson learned." • T models with an accessible text to make the thinking and languaging process clear for ST, so that they can transfer that thinking process to their own choice reading
7 10:00	T	• T sets up directions, so ST know what to do	7 10:00	T	
8 10:30	T	• ST build on each other's thinking	8 10:30	T	• Guided practice • "Practice this same process together" • ST 1 suggests another theme from chart
				ST	• Other ST agree with suggestion and rationale provided

Figure 4.2 Two field log notemaking examples from the same classroom observation *(Continued)*

11 ST 11:30	• T redirects groups that need help • ST seem productive in their groups	11 T 11:30	• T listens to ST and signals that listening through nonverbals (nodding head, taking notes about what ST say) and verbals ("Tell me more about what you mean by. ...") • Feedback not generic ("Good job"); specific to the lesson objective ("Okay, so what you're showing us through the evidence you're offering is how you had to build understanding of the issues and themes the texts explores across chapters. That's really important and skillful in explaining how you saw the emergence of a theme.") • Shares predetermined groups on screen so all ST feel included and don't have to be without a partner
12 T 15:30	• T offers feedback • T asks ST to return to the text to offer thinking and examples. Shows the importance of textual evidence for thinking	12 T 15:30	• Gives 2 min. warning to build ST ownership for decision-making and progress
13 T 20:30	• Establishes expectations for individual work	13 T 20:30 ST	• T visualizes the shared learning about how themes emerge, less than focuses on specific answers. This circulates power among ST as capable thinker and readers whose contributions matter for everyone's learning and understanding. • T calls into the conversation specific ST to emphasize the strength of their contributions to the group's thinking
14 T 25:30		14 T 25:30	
15 ST 26:00	• Focused on the task at hand • One ST stares out the window for long time	15 T 26:00	
16 T 27:00		16 ST 27:00	
17 T 29:00	• T is assessing ST while moving around the room. • Answers questions to clarify assignment	17 T 29:00	• Affirms a move that a ST is making well Reteaches, encourages the ST forward, or offers a challenge • It seems to me, the T is differentiating instruction live to meet STs' strengths and needs after listening rather than jumping to conclusions too quickly.

Figure 4.2 *(Continued)*

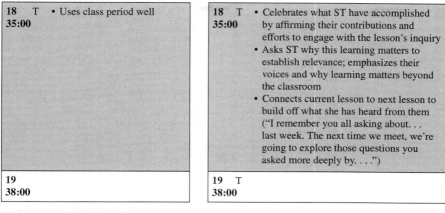

Figure 4.2 *(Continued)*

How Framework Lenses Influence Interpretations of Sticking Points

As we explored in Chapter Three, both logs focus on the classroom learning and teaching. Gabriel's notemaking interpretations, or framing, of those interactions, however, are differently focused, and those differences are largely informed by two different framework lenses for making meaning of the observations.

Classroom management offers a framework rationale for what Gabriel was focused on in Field Log A. Gabriel attends to how his mentor teacher runs the class, or how the class is "managed" by the teacher. For instance, in line one, Gabriel notes how students are "focused" and his mentor teacher "wasted [no] time getting into the lesson." Later, in line 13, Gabriel notes that she "establishes expectations for individual work," which supports students' ability to remain "focused on the task at hand" (line 15). In these instances, Gabriel is focused on student engagement and his mentor's effective use of time.

Gabriel's specific notemaking suggests that he is likely drawing on prevalent conversations about classroom management in educational discourse. Much of the feedback early career teachers receive is about how to keep students engaged in the work of the lesson with a focus on what teachers can do to keep students focused and on-task. We saw this play out in the case of the administrator who questioned the noise level in Cruz's classroom in Chapter Two. It's, therefore, no wonder observers might easily—and often, unknowingly—adopt such a lens through which to filter their interpretations of classroom observations and in so doing frame classroom interactions.

To be sure, unengaged students and ineffective use of class time are related and important. Without teachers' ability to notice and act in response to these noticings, students would not have the greatest chance of learning. For example, a management framework may illuminate why Gabriel makes special note in Field Log A of a student who "stares out the window for a long time" (line 15). This student may stand out to Gabriel because all other students are "focused." The flagging of this student's anomalous low engagement may indicate an emergent sticking point for Gabriel. The question, though, is why does low engagement matter to us as teachers, especially those with commitments to socially just ELA instruction? As the end goal, a classroom management framework doesn't prioritize larger considerations of equity, inclusion, and opportunity. Moreover, it doesn't offer a robust rationale for why engagement and use of time matter beyond compliance.

With the benefit of a socially just ELA instructional framework, in Field Log B Gabriel also makes notes about how his mentor teacher works to engage students (e.g., predetermining groups (line 11) and providing time warnings (line 12)), but Gabriel's notemaking serves a different interest and goal: how his mentor works to socially construct learning opportunities for students. Here, student engagement is an important intermediary step that supports the larger goal of shared and equitable learning opportunities for all students. In line three, for example, Gabriel considers how his mentor teacher invites students to consider how they and others socially construct meaning as they read popular texts like social media posts. In line 13, Gabriel notes how his mentor teacher "calls into the conversation specific students to emphasize the strength of their contributions to the group's thinking." By applying a socially just ELA instructional framework lens, Gabriel is framing interpretations with careful attention to the interactions between and among students and teacher, joint inquiry, and an emphasis on the language into and of the classroom, including how these moves allow power to circulate in support of shared learning.

☑ **4.1 Apply your understanding**

With the benefit of Gabriel's example field logs (see Figures 3.1 and 4.2), revisit a set of your field notes. Add notemaking to your field notes using your socially just ELA instructional framework lens. Pay particular attention to how you make visible your situated perspective as you make meaning of the classroom instruction and/or interactions. Use the prompts and guidance in Figure 4.1 to guide your notemaking.

4.2 Reflecting

After you've completed box 4.1, reflect in writing or with others on what you noticed in your notemaking. How is the process helping you frame sticking points that have emerged? Or is it? What do you need or want to continue to practice? To see? To understand about the process and what it makes visible?

To further solidify our understanding of how framing through our socially just ELA framework supports our interpretation of sticking points, let's turn to an example case.

Alexandra: Case Study

In the classroom where Alexandra was observing and learning, her mentor teacher introduced students to critical literary theory as tools for reading texts. In support of her mentor's overarching instructional goal, Alexandra explains her concentrated work with Randall, a student who was part of a small group with which Alexandra was interacting:

 4.3 Alexandra, in her own words

I was leading a small group discussion about students' connection between the gender lens and their choice reading. Before this point, we had already walked through the process with advertisements so that they could gain a better understanding of how to apply the lens to their young adult literature choice reading.

Alexandra had experience using ethnographic notetaking and making and was committed to enacting socially just ELA instruction. As a result, she sought to capture her interactions with students, because she knew that doing so would enable her to study how her choices to say or do certain things would open or foreclose opportunities for student learning. On this day, she pulled out her phone to audio record the small group interaction. (At this point in the semester, students in her mentor's classroom were quite familiar with this approach. Both Alexandra and her mentor had normalized conversations about how teachers study their teaching just like they ask students to study their language.) Later, Alexandra transcribed the exchange using (.) to indicate second pauses in speech:

RANDALL: I don't think there's that much I can do with this [lens].

ALEXANDRA: (.) What's your book called? What's it about?

RANDALL: There's this 14-year-old boy, who (.) uh (.) (looks at the back of the book) (.) So it's freezing cold outside and his father is lying dead next to him on the floor (.) and um a stranger shows up claiming that his father owes him money (.) and (.) so the kid (.)

ALEXANDRA: (nodding head to encourage him to keep going)

RANDALL: I haven't read that far into it but

ALEXANDRA: You read the back summary

RANDALL: (still staring at the back of the book)

ALEXANDRA: So

RANDALL: So I guess the whole thing is him trying to get to this place (.) there's not really (.) like (.)

ALEXANDRA: Ok, so would you say that the majority of the characters in this book are male then?

RANDALL: Yeah (.) all of them.

ALEXANDRA: Ok all of them, so for the first question you could talk about how there [are] only male characters in the book (Randall nods) and what does that mean, does it have anything to do with the books genre? (.) um would it be different if the characters were women? Do you think the story lines would be different or that you would read it in a different way if all the characters were women instead?

RANDALL: Yeah (.)

ALEXANDRA: So you could talk about that, you could talk about how (.) cause this book is um, is it like a thriller? (.) like is it (.) I don't want to say violent but like action packed?

RANDALL: I feel like (.) yeah there's action.

ALEXANDRA: So you could talk about how the book is revolving mainly around men, right? (Randall nods) and what the absence of the women characters kinda says about the genre itself like if that makes sense (.) does that help you?

RANDALL: I mean (.) kinda

Alexandra chose to transcribe this particular small group conversation in which only Randall was speaking, because she was aware of the emergence of a sticking point. She wanted her colleagues' help in thinking about how to navigate it in future teaching. The power of the transcript as a form of notetaking is that it enables notemaking interpretations based on the exact language used by both students and teacher—in this case her own language moves. As Alexandra reflected orally with colleagues, she engaged in note-making that gave her an opportunity to surface the sticking point:

☞ **4.4 Alexandra, in her own words**

I found myself struggling a little because I felt like I was pulling teeth to get students to talk. Looking back on the conversation and re-listening to the audio, I was concerned that Randall was just agreeing with me to get me to stop talking and that he truly didn't see the connection with his choice reading and the gender lens.

If I were to adjust or adapt my approach and had the chance to redo this lesson, one of the things I would change is giving Randall too much guidance. My sticking point was questioning when to stop the guiding, when to allow students to make these connections on their own while at the same time acknowledging that students may be struggling and realizing that they need guidance in applying the lens to texts. I under-stand that socially just ELA instruction tries to help students develop independence as thinkers, talkers, and readers. I see that I was doing too much here. I wasn't really building students' independence at all. I was talking for them.

Alexandra used the conversation with her colleagues as a notemaking space to explore the sticking point that emerged for her during this inter-action. She had the sense that students weren't engaged in the conver-sation as much as she had hoped. With the benefit of a socially just ELA instructional framework as a lens for viewing the conversation, Alexandra began to see the extent to which her dominance as the primary speaker in the "discussion" closed opportunities for students to rehearse their thinking about how to apply the gender lens to their readings. The sticking point, then, was that Alexandra valued building students' independent ability to apply the gender lens to their readings through dialogic teaching and learn-ing. However, her method—the way she facilitated the conversation—sup-ported more monologic, teacher-centric teaching that prioritized her talk over student talk (Juzwik et al., 2013). She noticed the sticking point, because she was able to study the conversation through her notetaking and because she had a clear vision for what socially just ELA instruction seeks to accomplish.

In Alexandra's case we see the power of notemaking through the lens of our socially just ELA framework, but we also see how it aids in teachers' ability to frame the sticking points that surface. Notably, Alexandra's concern about students' low-engagement differs from a management lens in that she reflects on the implications of Randall's ability to engage in the discussion for his own and his peers' learning through and because of the discussion. As she was teaching Alexandra felt uncomfortable with the way the discussion developed. She was frustrated by the lack of fluidity and engagement in the conversation. Her sense that she was "pulling teeth" made it hard for her to follow the plan she had developed, which was reliant on eager and ready student engagement. Her initial notetaking as she transcribed the interaction helped Alexandra begin notemaking and work to interpret from multiple perspectives what might have been going on in that interaction. This interconnected process supported Alexandra's ability to frame the sticking point as one about how she can develop the skills to facilitate and invite dialogic discussion between and among students, including Randall. This framing focused her attention on understanding how student engagement and interactions are directly reliant and supported by her ability to facilitate and prepare for class discussions in specific ways that would welcome and scaffold students' ability to join and, later, lead the conversation differently. As we'll see in the next chapter, this realization led Alexandra to further inquiry.

Like Alexandra, our ability to frame sticking points offers us a means to explore them further in order to determine how best to respond. Without efforts to interpret and frame sticking points, they can remain intangible and inaccessible, even invisible, resources for growing our understanding of how and why to enact socially just ELA instruction in the classroom cultures of which we are a part.

Reference

Juzwik, M. M., Borsheim-Black, C., Caughlan, S., & Heintz, A. (2013). *Inspiring dialogue: Talking to learn in the English classroom.* Teachers College Press.

5
Inquiring: Digging Deeper

Our interpretive work in framing sticking points invites us to dig deeper and consider what we need to understand or learn so that we can take informed action. As teachers, we're driven to action. We want to make things better. We want to serve all learners well. And yet we live in educational worlds that are often driven by a desire for quick fixes and solutions. At times, it can feel impossible or, at best, tricky to resist that push for swift change.

But those of us who understand the complicated systems we work within understand the danger of jumping to quick conclusions or hasty decisions. We know that the learners we support live complicated lives that influence

DOI: 10.4324/9781003134442-7

how they come to and experience learning in our classrooms. We, too, are complex people whose lives and identities necessarily shape our work and learning in classrooms. We know intuitively that when we pause and buy ourselves time to dig deeper with the aim of understanding from multiple perspectives, not just our own, we come to richer insights.

Without the ability to account for these complexities through intentional inquiry, to understand those factors at work in our interactions, we risk implementing changes and simple solutions that aren't responsive to the people and places that shape our classroom cultures. Think about a time when you, like me, thought to yourself, "Knowing what I know now, I would have done that differently." Hitting pause to delve deeper enables us to make decisions that support our ability to speak more specifically, compellingly, and sustainably to the sticking points that emerge in the unique classroom contexts and interactions of which we are a part.

Alexandra: Case Study, Continued

Alexandra's case and the sticking point that emerged as Randall struggled to see the applicability of a gender lens in his choice reading from Chapter Four makes clearer how framing sticking points naturally ignites a desire to inquire further. Alexandra's notemaking began to reveal questions about her own ability to facilitate discussion:

☞ 5.1 Alexandra, in her own words

Later in the lesson I realized that the real dilemma for Randall was the absence of women in his choice reading, which left him confused about how to apply the gender lens to his reading of that text. He thought that conversations about gender were only really about women, and if there weren't female characters, then there wasn't much to say.

When thinking about how I can address this sticking point in future lessons, I could ask students to rehearse their thinking with either partners or small groups so that they have another person to bounce wonderings with. I also think about the importance of my language and how I chose to set up these questions. For example, during this conversation I realized that the way I phrased my questions simply asked for one-word responses. For example, during my conversation instead of asking, "Does the absence of women say anything?" I could word it differently to say, "What does the absence of women suggest about dominant gender norms?" This would allow the students to think more in-depth about what the absence of women truly means. If I were to just re-phrase my questions, students could maybe go more in-depth in their responses.

I think finding the line between guiding and giving is a line that is hard and frustrating. As teachers, we just want students to understand so badly that we get too carried away and end up doing the thinking for them without even knowing.

However, with small things like opening up for discussion, re-phrasing the questions, having them work with other classmates, we can let students develop the thinking, and we can truly support them into that thinking, rather than telling.

Alexandra's wondering prompted her to explore first what may have been causing students confusion or difficulty as they worked to apply the gender lens to their readings. In her reflection, we see that Alexandra has learned through further observation and interactions during the lesson that students' misunderstandings about the gender lens and what it enables readers to examine may have caused confusion that prevented them from knowing what to say in response to her many prompts. In turn, this realization led Alexandra to see a need to clarify for students how analysis of gender is not solely focused on female identifying characters. She also realized how her use of right-there questions—those that solicited right, wrong, one-word responses—may have discouraged students from fully engaging in the conversation she was seeking to foster. Paired with one another, Alexandra felt, these adjustments might create space for students to engage in the conversation more successfully and eagerly in order to offer possible interpretations that result from the application of the gender lens to their readings, even those without the presence of female characters. Her reflections establish a line of inquiry for further exploration in her future interactions with her mentor teacher or field instructor. In those conversations, she might explore whether and how to act on these possibilities for learning from student responses during her teaching.

Tools for Delving Deeper

Inquiry Questions: Seeing and Learning More

As Alexandra makes clear, framing sticking points prompts us toward further observation and classroom engagement where we can consider student and teacher interactions, our own situated perspective, and the possibility that we will always have more to learn about what it means to and how we enact socially just English language arts (ELA) instruction. Developing inquiry threads and questions alongside our notemaking encourages us to wonder rather than assuming that our understandings are the only interpretative readings of the sticking points we encounter. As we seek to learn from our continued observations and, by association, the perspectives and understandings of those we are observing and with whom we are interacting, we come to more fully capture the ways in which others see the same experiences and interactions. Figure 5.1 offers an overview of the inquiry questioning process. If all teaching is a draft, then developing inquiry questions and opportunities through our observations can serve as an especially important tool for continually growing our teaching in support of learners and socially just ELA.

Let's revisit Field Log B from earlier chapters to see what inquiry questioning affords us as we journey forward in ongoing classroom observation, interaction, and teaching. Figure 5.2 includes the inquiry questions that emerged from Gabriel's notetaking (see Figure 3.1) and making (see Figure 4.2) with a socially just ELA instructional frame. These questions reveal his eagerness to understand how his mentor teacher's actions and instructional choices support inclusive, equitable learning for all students. The questions also mark Gabriel's understanding that seeking clarity about the framework and rationales that inform his mentor teacher's actions and decisions have direct implications for Gabriel's future teaching and instructional decision-making, too.

Ethnographic approach	**Our goal** Wonderings based on observations **What we wonder about** What questions emerge for me that help me grow my teaching practice?
+ Socially just ELA framework lens	**Our goal** Identifying questions that I need to explore further in order to understand the insider perspectives of teachers and students in a particular classroom culture **What else we wonder about** • What questions would help me understand what motivates or informs teacher and student actions or talk? • What more about the instructional decisions, students' lived experiences, and/or classroom cultural norms do I need to understand in order to make data-informed interpretations? • How might I rewrite my initial notemaking interpretations as inquiry questions for further investigation and observation? • How might the exploration of these questions inform my ability to understand how students and teachers' interactions in this classroom context can inform how I find entrances for enacting socially just ELA instruction in this or other classroom cultures?

Figure 5.1 Inquiring

Line Time	Speaker	Inquiry Questions
1	T	• I wonder how "I can" objectives open opportunities for ST to see themselves differently than other kinds of objective statements that de-center ST or that make less clear the work of the lesson.
2 :30	T	
3 1:00	T	• How does the T build on knowledge of STs' lived experiences in this conversation, and how does the T's effort to do so invite STs differently into the classroom inquiry?
4 2:00	T	• How does the T use direct instruction differently here to share tools that ST see as essential for supporting their efforts to engage in a meaningful inquiry task? (A working theory/wondering: The issue of engagement is a non-issue here, because the T has established clear relevance that builds on STs' lived experiences and questions as readers.)
5 5:00	T	• What is it about the banking model of education that makes me surprised to see some of these moves and how they make possible STs' ability to access and engage with meaningful learning here?
6 5:30	T	• How is it that modeling opens opportunities for ST to try out the thinking necessary to articulate how themes emerge and why we as readers care about themes—what they do for us?
7 10:00	T	
8 10:30	T	• How can Ts use their feedback for multiple purposes: to help ST adjust their ability to take on and try out the lesson objective, to build community, to help ST take risks that make learning possible, to help ST save face and not compromise their social status among peers, to celebrate ST thinking and emerging understanding? If I understand my feedback to be working on multiple levels, then how does that help me develop the multilayered ways in which my feedback serves many ST, not just those I'm talking directly with and to?
11 13:30	ST	
12 15:30	T	• How does a T's choice to circulate among ST during work time position them differently in relation to ST (as opposed to asking ST to raise their hands or come to the T's desk)?
13 20:30	T ST	
14 25:30	T	
15 26:00	T	
16 27:00	ST	
17 29:00	T	• How do I develop the skill of being able to assess live, in-the-moment how ST are enacting the lesson objective so that my feedback is tailored to meet ST needs and strengths, which motivates them to keep going?
18 35:00	T	• What are the range of language moves that T use to wrap up a lesson while accomplishing related goals: setting up the next lesson, affirming ST voices, linking to previous lessons and learning, building ST synthesis, etc.?
19 38:00		

Figure 5.2 Field log B inquiry questioning

You may have noticed how some of Gabriel's questions are specifically about his mentor teacher's instructional decisions (e.g., line 5) whereas other questions zoom out and pose possibilities for Gabriel's own future teaching and classroom interactions (e.g., line 17). Inquiry questions are, therefore, about what we're seeing and how we're understanding what we're seeing as well as about how what we're seeing invites us to consider our own teaching practice and interactions. In other words, observation and interaction becomes a space to reflect on what others are doing as much as on what we are doing or will do in our own instruction. Inquiry questions that take this dual approach to wondering and delving deeper in the moment and for the future support our ability to negotiate sticking points today and tomorrow.

Recursive Relationships Among Notetaking, Notemaking, and Inquiry Questioning

Although it might be easy to conclude that notetaking, notemaking, and inquiry questioning occur as a linear process, this is not always the case. Alexandra's case also highlights how the tools of notetaking, notemaking, and inquiry questioning are useful interanimating resources for negotiating sticking points. Her recursive use of these tools further emphasizes how, for example, notemaking and inquiry questioning can and should prompt further notetaking that lends clarity to the nature of the sticking points we encounter. Together, notemaking, notetaking, and inquiring combined with a clear framework lens distill when and why sticking points emerge for us as we work to teach for justice.

With careful practice, these tools can support a recursive revisiting and rethinking of our observations and classroom interactions whereby, for instance, our notemaking can give rise to inquiry questions that prompt us to return to our noticing with further notetaking. Our inquiry questioning can encourage us to consider why something happened, which invites us into notemaking, for instance. What's key here is that we remain aware of what we're doing as we observe and what our observation is in service of.

☑ **5.2 Apply your understanding**

Revisit the field notetaking and making you've previously recorded. Add to that thinking inquiry questions that surface genuine wonderings you have about both what you're seeing and how it has implications for your future teaching and instruction. Use Figure 5.1 to guide your inquiry questioning.

Then, annotate your questions to identify possibilities for beginning to explore your inquiry questions. Which questions might you answer through your ongoing observations? Which ones might best be answered through conversations with a mentor teacher or student(s)? Are there questions that you can solicit another perspective in grappling with possible ways of seeing or understanding that sticking point?

☑ 5.3 Apply your understanding

If you have applied your understanding in Chapter Two, box 2.7, by researching more about the context where you will be or are engaged in fieldwork, revisit what you discovered. Take notice of the inquiry questions you posed there. Then, consider what you wrote in relation to box 5.2. To what extent are your wonderings filtered through your own perspective, lived experiences, and identities? What, if any, opportunities do you now see to make visible your situated perspective as you seek to inquire further? Make note of this new thinking in annotations to what you originally wrote or thought for box 2.7. Does this new thinking reveal new lines of inquiry or affirm things you would benefit from learning about the systems (e.g., school districts) and contexts (e.g., larger communities, classroom cultures) that shape your fieldwork?

5.4 Reflecting

After you've completed box 5.2 and/or 5.3, reflect in writing or with others on what you noticed in your inquiry questions and annotations. How is the process helping you zoom in to learn more that might help you understand more fully the nature of the sticking points you're noticing? Or is it? What do you need or want to continue to practice? To see? To understand about the process and what it makes visible?

Joint Inquiry: The Need to Invite Others' Noticing

If we return to Alexandra's case, there's another important factor at play, and it helps to underscore how inquiry is a recursive process for zooming in to explore further the nature of the sticking point. Alexandra was eager to transcribe and share her interaction and associated sticking point with her colleagues because she valued their insights and ability to think with her about how to proceed. This belief in the value of collegial inquiry is aligned with her socially just ELA instructional framework, which posits that learning occurs through social interactions. Just as social interactions shape classroom learning, social interactions also shape our professional learning. Alexandra trusted that, because her colleagues articulated framework commitments to socially just ELA instruction, they would be able to help her contemplate the sticking point that emerged in her classroom interaction with students.

Sometimes we're led to believe, or it can at least feel, that classroom observations and, by extension, sticking point negotiation, are individual tasks meant to serve us alone. Alexandra's case gives us reason to question this assumption. Alexandra's initial notetaking was done independently; she was engaged in an interaction first and foremost with her own teaching. In some ways this process is like our reading of a text.

On one hand, reading a book, for example, can feel like an independent practice. On the other hand, though, we recognize that all interactions with texts involve others—whether they are physically present in the moment or not. After all, our reading of a text invites us into an interaction with at least one other's thoughts, ideas, and creations. So, too, is this true of our observation in classrooms. Most commonly, we are collecting our thoughts and engaging in notetaking independently. However, we are doing so as a form of interaction with what we are seeing, experiencing, feeling, thinking, and so on. The act of notetaking, notemaking, and inquiry questioning is a social interaction with the classroom in which we are observing and participating.

For Alexandra, as for many of us, that interaction invites us to immediately consider future interactions in the same and other classrooms. Our noticing of dissonance, of sticking points, should prompt us to consider the implications of our observations and what they make visible and, therefore, possible in future classroom teaching and interactions.

Nonetheless, thus far I've emphasized our role as primary observers and noticers. What happens, then, when, even if we use these tools, we don't notice something? If we return to the acknowledgment that we are situated beings who, therefore, have particular perspectives, then this reality invites us to, as Alexandra did, solicit others' help in observing the same classroom cultures. Other people's noticing eyes offer alternate perspective that can, at times, prompt us to wonder and notice differently. What is more, if those colleagues share framework orientations with us, then their noticings can deepen our own ability to see dissonance where our own biases may otherwise cloud our vision.

Darius and Colleagues: Case Study

The power of colleagues' noticing eyes became apparent to Darius in his debriefing about a lesson he had just taught. As colleagues were sharing what they appreciated about Darius's lesson, they referred to the opening of the lesson when in passing Darius calls students "my besties," a short form of best friends. During the conversation, colleagues chimed in to affirm and then complicate this choice:

FIONNA: Saying 'hey besties' at the beginning felt like a really inclusive way of getting the class engaged and feeling like they have a connection with a teacher.

MARTHA: Bouncing off that, it also makes for a very comfortable environment. If any students do feel confused about instructions, they're more likely to ask for help.

DIRK: Let's read that from a different angle. It might work for a lot of us that way. But put yourself in the shoes of a student who doesn't find school an inclusive and welcoming space. How might 'besties' be read differently or position some students differently than we're talking about right now?

DEONTE: I think if we're looking at it through that lens, it almost becomes an artificial gesture to bring people in. So, it's like saying, this is because I want you to feel connected, even if we don't really have a bond like that. And then the other thing with that is that it could also ostracize the students who may not be vocal with their participation in class with the teacher. It's like the more students who interact with the teacher or associate themselves with the teacher get the 'bestie' tag where people who don't might not. It's an intricate balance there, I suppose.

DIRK: Yeah. It's complicated because what we heard is that it works for some people. But we also need to be, especially as socially just ELA instructors, very careful about who we're inviting in and who we might be simultaneously and unintentionally excluding with a simple move like calling students 'besties.' We might be saying to some students, to do well in this class, you have to be my bestie. What about a student who doesn't feel the need or desire to be our bestie?

CLAUDIA: I'm going to play devil's advocate to your devil's advocate, Dirk. If we're looking at it through that lens and we're thinking about how we all need to be really careful about what we say, because of students who don't feel that school is a warm and welcoming environment, then who's to say that everybody could say that they don't feel welcome, no matter what we say?

DIRK: In all things in teaching, don't we have to make the best choice? I'm thinking about teachers that I've heard refer to their students as 'scholars,' which feels different. I might have a student who says, 'I don't feel like a scholar today.' But calling students 'scholars' puts them in a different relationship with me as a teacher. Scholar suggests that we're in an academic community, in an intellectual and professional relationship to one another. There's a really careful balance and difference there between telling students you have to share a friendly, personal relationship with me versus I'm welcoming you into an intellectual, professional relationship, which doesn't mean that you have to like me as a best friend.

At first Fionna and Martha offer notemaking comments about what they see as the effectiveness of a language move to call students 'besties.' Then, Dirk raises an inquiry question, which presents the group with a sticking point for further consideration. Is it socially just to call students 'besties,' Dirk wonders? By posing this sticking point Dirk invites the group to read 'besties' with different noticing eyes.

Dirk's sticking point question creates space for others to join the conversation. Deonte extends Dirk's noticing. Deonte suggests the group consider the way 'bestie' positions students in relationship to the teacher. In his effort to note that a decision about whether to use 'bestie' requires an "intricate balance," Deonte complicates the group's initial thinking and opens further opportunities to consider the balance in relation to the group's commitment to socially just ELA instruction. Dirk builds on Deonte's thoughts and effort to bring the group back to their shared and evolving understanding of socially just ELA instruction to help make the decision. At the same time, Claudia's comments suggest that she finds the group a safe place to question further by raising a potential counterargument for shared inquiry.

Together, the colleagues try out different insider perspectives, or noticing eyes, to read the language choice. Later in the conversation, the group considers if there are classroom cultures where 'bestie' would be an inclusive term of affection for students as they consider the unique classroom community within which Darius was teaching, a classroom community that the colleagues shared experience working within.

As his colleagues contemplate the sticking point, Darius listens. That Darius didn't feel compelled to interject justification or explanation for the choice (although presumably he would have been welcomed to do so), says something about the safety and possibility of the group's inquiry. The group debrief wasn't aimed at solving a problem or even creating a problem that needs solving. Instead, Darius's teaching and interactive choices offer the group a shared text for reflecting on their collective efforts to enact socially just ELA instruction. It raises questions and offers a space for shared thinking. The group values their shared ability to surface multiple perspectives rather than definitively answer what Darius or anyone else ought to do in response.

For the larger part of the conversation, Darius chooses to listen to the conversation and quietly contemplate what's being said. At the end of the conversation, though, he adds:

☞ **5.5 Darius, in his own words**

I just want to say how appreciative I am of the feedback that you all gave. You build my wonderings. You presented so many different ideas that I had not thought about, and now I'm excited to go back and be like, "Okay, let's change this up. Let's do this." So, yes, I'm just very appreciative of this experience. Thank you all.

Significantly, Darius did not bring the sticking point to the group. Rather, the group's conversation about Darius's teaching made visible a sticking point that Darius hadn't considered or hadn't immediately seen. Yet, Darius's last words suggest he valued that the sticking point had emerged through the group's inquiry into his teaching as well as its implications for others' teaching.

Darius's case, thus, affirms the importance of colleagues who share framework commitments and who are comfortable serving as noticing eyes for us. Their noticing, interpreting, and wondering can reveal sticking points where we might not otherwise see them. And where colleagues see supportive inquiry into emergent sticking points as mutually beneficial, everyone stands to gain from the ability to frame and inquire into sticking points together.

Of course, we don't always have ready access to a group of colleagues who share framework understanding and commitments. When we do not have ready access to a group, we can still inquire with a single colleague within or beyond our context, as we'll revisit in Chapters Nine and Ten.

Whether we have a group, a single colleague, or no immediate colleagues to engage in conversation, by developing specific listening skills that enable us to involve others as we inquire, we can strengthen our understanding of emergent sticking points and insider perspectives. These special ways of listening will be the focus of our exploration in the next chapter.

6
Radical Listening: Learning Where Others Are Coming From

Being a good teacher requires being a good listener. That might strike you as the most self-evident statement of the century. But let's pause for a moment and consider whether and how we've learned to become "good" listeners, especially in relation to our instructional practice. Although English language arts (ELA) standards and curricula talk about the value of teaching and learning to read, write, speak, and listen (and increasingly view), few of us have ever received dedicated instruction focused on *how* to listen. It's assumed that because for many auditorily abled people, we begin life hearing, we pick up listening as we go. But, if you really think about it, that's not necessarily the case for anyone.

DOI: 10.4324/9781003134442-8

In Chapters Four and Five, we met Alexandra who realized that there's skill required to effectively solicit student thinking so that socially just ELA teachers can truly listen to students as they co-construct understanding. Similarly, in Chapter Five, Darius and his colleagues eagerly listened to one another's interpretations of "bestie" in order to identify possible language options for future classroom interactions. In each of these cases, teacher candidates were actively engaged in **radical listening**, a form of active engagement with what and who we're hearing in instructional interactions.

The need for radical listening in our professional interactions with students, colleagues, families, and school leadership follows from our ability to identify lines of inquiry through our notetaking and making. Our desire to delve deeper into the nature of the sticking points we face in our teaching and professional interactions invites us into a different kind of active listening relationship with others. I propose that this stance is radical because although it may seem self-evident, it's not as common as we might expect in classroom and school communities. It cannot be taken for granted. Rather, it's radical because it requires our commitment to continually cultivate listening of the sort we'll discuss in this chapter.

I'm an amateur yogi (one who practices yoga) at best. I'll spare you the visual imagery. Let me just say that my practice is rarely pretty. I'm humbled by my limits as I try out new poses that require me to differently contort my body. I quest for balance. But I often wobble. I stumble. I fall. Yet, I'm reassured by my mentors that this is a necessary and important part of listening to my body. Without practice, without a willingness to stumble and fall, and perhaps most importantly, without a willingness to return with renewed commitment to the process, I cannot journey. I will arrive no further ahead.

Radical listening is similar. It's a practice that requires an inclination to fumble toward deeper understanding. It benefits greatly from our willingness to return to classroom communities and interactions with renewed commitment to the people and the process. Sticking points bubble up through our teaching and learning with other people. Without efforts to seek understanding of where those other people are coming from through listening during ongoing interactions, we miss opportunities to better understand the nature of our own sticking points so that we can be in better relationship with those with whom we learn and grow. In other words, we do little to honor and mine the riches that listening reveals if we do not pause to take stock of what we've learned from others about the frameworks that inform their decision-making and interactions. Without that knowledge, it's tough to act in relation to and, importantly, *with* students, mentors, and colleagues.

Listening Versus Hearing

Distinct from hearing, listening is an interactional process of meaning-making. Often, we think about listening as a unidirectional, passive process. If you've ever found yourself in a large lecture hall or attending a speaking event, you know that culturally your job is to remain quiet as you take in what's being said. The unspoken emphasis is really more on hearing than on listening. Ultimately, you get to choose whether you really listen—whether you choose to actively process and engage with the content and ideas you're hearing.

To be real, it's human nature to find ourselves mentally adrift in these situations, too. Have you found yourself intending to listen when unconsciously the speaker's voice becomes a litany of blurred sounds like the teacher's voice in Peanuts cartoons? Clearly articulated words can easily become "blah, blah, blah, wah, wah, wah" in the space of our minds as we turn to other thoughts. We're hearing but not really listening. At least once or twice (or in my case, too many times to count), you may recall parents, guardians, or teachers questioning, "Do you even hear me?" Really, those well-intentioned mentors should have asked, "Were you really listening to me?" At least in my experience, the honest truth is "no," but there's too much at stake to answer honestly: "I heard you, but I wasn't listening."

In the case of reading, it is for this very reason that many of us have learned or been taught to rely on annotating as we read complex texts that require our careful attention. The work of annotating keeps us engaged and interacting with what's being said. Listening to what's being said, like annotating what's been written, requires a set of skills for attending to and processing what we're hearing.

For those of us committed to socially just ELA instruction, developing our skill as listeners helps us calibrate what's possible in teaching and learning interactions. Listening helps us understand and assess before responding. Our listening enables us to study and comprehend how others use their language with rhetorical awareness of and responsiveness to different audiences and situations. It is key to fostering particular kinds of relationships with students and, by extension, with colleagues, families, and others who support the students with whom we work and learn. It's all a part of the co-construction of learning that occurs through discourse—our own and, importantly for the purposes of socially just ELA instruction and this chapter, others. In the end, radical listening helps us contemplate how we choose to respond to emergent sticking points, because we care about maintaining and fostering ongoing relationships with others.

What's Radical About Listening?

Knowing that the term "radical" used to describe people can connote admiration or condemnation, you might pause to wonder what it means to be a radical listener and whether that's a disposition to which you aspire. Here I mean to demark radical listening as counterculture in many schools and classroom communities where the traditional framework for listening really stands in for hearing. If we are really talking about affecting systemic change of the sort that socially just ELA instruction calls us to enact, then we must be willing to overhaul our assumptions about what is meant by listening.

You likely have thought about how many hours students will spend in your classroom and with you, especially in relation to the hours students will spend with other adults in their lives, including their own parents, guardians, or relatives. I was reminded of this early in my teaching career when a parent concerned about her student's academic progress in my ELA class remarked, "Listen, he sees you more each day than he sees me. I work late hours. He practices football and then goes to work. We both get home exhausted. When we do talk, it's usually about what he hasn't done or needs to do. I just don't know what to do to get him to do his work or to understand why he needs to graduate." My heart broke a bit as this deeply committed parent shared how she felt helpless in supporting her student, despite her eagerness to see him succeed.

Listening required something much different from me than would have been required if I chose just to hear her words. Listening called me to action. It called me into the sticking point we were both negotiating from different vantage points as we both worked to support this student in different ways with different resources. Layer on a commitment to a socially just ELA instructional framework, and you can see how I realized that I didn't have a choice about whether to listen or hear that mom. If I truly was committed to opening opportunities for learning for this mom's son, then I needed to listen. And, listening invited me to understand the sticking point source for this mom and for her son, too. I began to understand differently what may be posing roadblocks to this student's success. Listening invited me to reply, but not with quick solutions. In the end, I would work with her and with her son differently, but first I needed to acknowledge what I had heard—the byproduct of my listening. In fact, I would argue, jumping immediately to suggest potential solutions to this sticking point we shared would have negated the whole project of radical listening. She deserved to verify that I had truly processed what she was sharing. She, like all people, wanted to be sure that I at least was attempting to understand where she was coming from, how she read the sticking point, and what she knew about her son that I could never fully begin to understand without her help. She wanted to know that we were both reading "What's going on here?" similarly before we could attempt to move forward together. Jumping to solutions, while it might seem like a way of honoring what we hear, risks making premature interpretative judgments and assumptions about where others are coming from and what they intend by their words and actions.

It's this stance—this willingness to initially resist our helping urge long enough to verify that we hear what someone is sharing through their words or actions is what they intend—that I'm suggesting is radical and so critically necessary as a part of our efforts to negotiate sticking points—our own and those, like this mom's, that people surface for and with us. Radical listening requires a commitment to living differently and intentionally in the classrooms that mentors and colleagues humbly and generously invite us into so that we can enter our own classrooms ready to assume a radical listening stance that honors those with whom we work. It's that stance, as the cases in this chapter will also show, that opens more meaningful and sustainable opportunities to negotiate sticking points while maintaining and deepening our relationships with others. To be clear, it's not that radical listening can serve as some sort of magical elixir that ensures that everyone gets along well and works in support of shared frameworks. Rather, radical listening helps us consider, weigh, and later act in ways that intentionally enable us to act in support of our commitments to socially just ELA instruction without jeopardizing our relationships with others and, importantly, our future ability to remain and grow as teachers for justice.

 6.1 **Reflecting**

Think about times or experiences that you have had in school as a student or as a teacher where you genuinely felt heard. What was it about those moments or interactions that made you feel heard and understood? Use these reflections as a chance to begin curating your own list of radical listening strategies. How might you want to employ similar strategies in your own teaching or professional interactions?

Natalie and Kevin: A Case Study

Natalie and Kevin shared a mentor teacher in their clinical experience. Working in the same classroom meant that they shared knowledge of the same students and could, therefore, explore shared sticking points with the benefit of their common observations and interactions.

Their mentor teacher recently introduced the gender lens and asked students to apply it to their reading of various texts. Early in these introductory efforts, and not unlike Alexandra, Natalie and Kevin both observed and interacted with students in small groups as they worked to apply the critical lens to their reading of works of fiction. They worked alongside their mentor teacher to dispel misconceptions and help students understand how the gender lens supports reader analysis of diverse representations of gendered identities, including characters who consider their gender to be influx or fluid.

Beyond the introduction and application of the gender lens, their mentor teacher also chose to strategically book talk new young adult literature titles that included diverse representations of gender expression and identities as well as sexual identities. Aware that the school and local community did not afford much space for students to engage in conversations or develop language for understanding how to talk in gender expansive and inclusive ways as well as that there were students in her classes who felt unsafe sharing their own identities across gender and sex identity spectra, Natalie and Kevin's mentor also made a point to model through her book talks how to effectively engage in and employ representative and respectful language that honors the diverse ways in which people identify. Their mentor never explicitly invited students to comment on or engage in book talks. Rather, she used these as impromptu moments to model and, as she shared with Kevin and Natalie, "plant seeds for other work we do and for later down the road."

Even within this classroom community guided by a strong mentor teacher, sticking points emerged for Natalie and Kevin in their interactions with students. Kevin first gave voice to his sticking point in relation to one-on-one conferences with students who were working on blog posts. Their mentor used student blogging as a space to develop students' writerly identities and audience awareness across the school year. Each student chose a theme for their blog and then periodically contributed entries. As Kevin reflected on these conferences, he shared:

☞ 6.2 Kevin, in his own words

I was talking with students about their blog posts. One student I met was writing about things he hates and showed me his writing about hating the idea of being gender-fluid and similar non-binary ideas about gender. He went as far as to make fun of it and high-five a classmate sitting across from him…. Students were dehumanizing those who identify as non-binary or gender fluid. How do I approach these types of conversations and ideas without students immediately disregarding me as being insane, or against what they have been taught to believe in?

Natalie nodded in agreement and shared how she noticed "some real homophobic tendencies" in student comments in small groups, especially. As ELA teachers committed to social justice, these comments concerned both Natalie and Kevin. They both expressed eagerness to address gender and sexual discrimination through their instruction, especially as they recognized the very real physical and emotional threats to students who may have wished to identify in non-normative ways within the school culture.

As Natalie reflected on her observations, she weighed a number of different things. She explained her commitment to developing students' awareness of how their language can perpetuate discriminatory stereotypes and hate speech—both intentionally and unintentionally. She was mindful that, as her mentor shared, in other required coursework students had not been given direct instruction or opportunities to learn about diverse gender expressions and identities as well as sexual orientations. Additionally, Natalie surmised, the challenge was made more difficult because students had few, if any, interactions with those who identify differently than they do. Natalie reflected on her own experiences of schooling, which never prompted her to consider her own positionality and social privilege as a cisgendered, heterosexual female. She was also fully aware of and appreciative that a number of her colleagues working in the school identified as gender-fluid and genderqueer, and she felt confident that even in a smaller school, there were plenty of students who identified in non-normative ways but for whom the school environment made it unsafe to identify as they desired.

In response to her own and Kevin's reflections on their observations and interactions with students, Natalie took a leap in her instructional choices. With the support of her mentor teacher, she introduced a queer lens during some of the small group conversations she was facilitating as a way of helping students "consider intersectional identities, especially between gender and sexual orientation." During one small group meeting, Natalie used an excerpt from "Molly's Lips," a short story by Dahlia Adler (2018) in which, as Natalie explained to colleagues, "a young, closeted lesbian and her best friend realize they're in love." In a three-minute, small group discussion that followed the reading, Natalie found herself navigating this ongoing sticking point head on:

NATALIE: So, having read that passage, I'm just curious about your initial reactions. Anything at all. Is this something you're familiar with? Is it something you're comfortable with? Have you read anything like this before?

MAX: I'm not really comfortable with all that stuff.

NATALIE: Totally understandable, because it's something we don't talk about a lot, right?

MAX: I-uh-personally, I don't, uh, I don't believe in those types of things.

NATALIE: Yeah, and that's, uh, that's the value of this lens. So, what I'm hoping you can do is be open to considering something, be open to thinking about something; (.) that doesn't mean you approve, right?

MAX: I haven't really, you know, put much thought into it.

NATALIE: Yeah.

MAX: I haven't (...) I haven't really talked to someone who is like that so I've never had to put myself in that situation.

NATALIE: Yeah, so with that in mind, going to the third question here: "'Imagine yourself a'" —oh no, that's supposed to say "'as someone.'" Dang it, I thought I proofread this!— "'AS someone of a different gender and/or sexual orientation reading this, How do you think you would feel about it?'" So I guess that's the question here. (.) (to Max) I'm getting the impression that you are A) identifying as a man and B) identifying as straight. Do you think you would read this differently if you were not both of those things?

MAX: I mean if I was not both of those things I'd probably like this text.

NATALIE: Right, yeah.

MAX: But I am, you know, so. (.) Me being who I am I'm not really a big fan of it.

NATALIE: Yeah.

MAX: I'm not trying to be rude or anything (.) I'm just trying to express myself.

NATALIE: No, yeah, you're not being rude. That's what these discussions are for, right? I think you have to be honest.

Later, in a conversation with colleagues, Natalie posed an inquiry question that paralleled the one Kevin posed in their earlier conversation:

☞ **6.3 Natalie, in her own words**

I'm wondering, what's the best way to discuss sensitive, identity-related topics with students that sustains an environment supportive to minoritized and marginalized students while still giving privileged students the opportunity to voice their thoughts (if voicing thoughts is necessary for them to reflect and grow)? It is difficult enacting social justice in a classroom that has actively resistant students, especially to non-normative gender identities and sexual orientations, rather than students who are just unfamiliar with certain issues or unpracticed in discussing them.

I attempted to reframe things by asking Max to just consider without necessarily accepting. I tried to keep him engaged with the lesson, in part because dialogue is essential to learning, and if I can't get him engaged *at all*, I've certainly failed. However, I still question whether or not I should have (rather than immediately tried to reframe and redirect) engaged him a bit further in that conversation.

Natalie's sticking point and reflections here reveal a fundamentally related question: When do we interject, and when do we listen as we work to negotiate sticking points?

Natalie *was* listening to Max, even as she questioned whether she should have listened more extensively before reacting or responding. She had created a space where Max felt he could voice his own uncertainties and questions, and that she felt was "a small victory:"

☞ **6.4 Natalie, in her own words**

It wasn't all bad. Hearing Max acknowledge that, if he weren't a straight man, he would have appreciated the text seems like a small victory. I'm also pleased he felt comfortable sharing his thoughts with me.

What Natalie implicitly realizes is that listening takes time. Listening requires a willingness to allow people to use their talk to raise uncertainty in order to work toward understanding.

At the same time, listening also offers us space to better understand the frameworks that inform others' contributions and actions. As we listen, we solicit others' thinking and resist the urge to jump to snap judgments or assumptions about where they are coming from and where they have the potential to arrive.

Max's comment, "I haven't really talked to someone who is like that so I've never had to put myself in that situation," offered Natalie critical insight into what motivated Max's dismissal of the story and the queer lens. He lacked personal interactions with LGBTQIA+ identifying people, and he believed that if he could not personally identify with a character (or person), then the story offered him little. These understandings offer concrete and clear foundational understandings from which to make future instructional decisions.

Had she interjected or corrected Max, instead of listening, Natalie may have closed the door on an opportunity to understand Max's comments. Instead, Natalie's listening yielded Max's comments, which created an opening for her to consider where this revelation might lead in terms of his ability to take up the lens. When she says, "I'm getting the impression that you are A) identifying as a man and B) identifying as straight. Do you think you would read this differently if you were not both of those things?" she begins to explore with him his own identity as both a reader and human. As Natalie listens further, Max comments, "I'm just trying to express myself." For Natalie, this listening creates a space for her to more fully understand where Max is coming from. What Max reveals is that he, too, may be working to articulate, to develop language, for articulating his own gender expression and sexual orientation. In fact, his comment, in Natalie's mind, made clearer potential next steps:

☞ 6.5 Natalie, in her own words

When Max said that he'd never "talked to someone who is like that," should I have pointed out that, in all likelihood, he *does* know someone who identifies as queer—but just not openly or to him? I mean, isn't it the case that an estimated 5% of the US population is gay, so in all of the thousands of people he's met in his life, statistically at *least* one was not a cisgender and/or heterosexual person. Either way, I want to think about how this opening reveals a future opportunity to get the group, including Max, thinking about the social structures that shape LGBTQ+ identities. I know it takes time to earn students' trust and offer a wide variety of representations of LGBTQ+ peoples so the students can empathize and understand the complexity of what we're discussing.

One of the big takeaways for me personally was that students, Max included, need the *language* to discuss sensitive, identity-related topics. Those conversations happen so rarely in everyday life—at least for students that age—that the act of discussion itself is probably new and uncomfortable. Learning the language needed to discuss and have appropriate discussions modeled for them can potentially make all the difference between a productive, supportive discussion and one that is either hurtful or unfruitful.

Natalie's willingness to listen fully to Max made possible her understanding of why the lenses she and her mentor teacher were introducing to students posed real sticking points for Max, especially because he perceived the gender and queer lenses as an afront to his frameworks for self-identification and also for reading. He assumed that finding reading productive and instructive is predicated on being able to relate to it, just as he assumed that being able to relate to a person is predicated on being able to identify similarly. For Natalie, the opportunity to listen made clearer not only where Max was coming from and what was posing a sticking point for him in the group's learning and interactions but also ways of potentially negotiating her related instructional sticking point.

Tools for Learning to Radically Listen

Radical listening is premised on a belief that we can all learn to listen better. Strengthening our radical listening is an ongoing effort that benefits from regular practice—whether we're beginning or veteran teachers. Doing so requires a commitment to developing awareness of how we communicate as we listen. What messages do we send as we're listening to a speaker? Do those messages signal our engagement and investment in understanding what it is that speakers are saying and risking to share with us? As we begin to reflect on questions such as these and the positions we assume as listeners, we begin to recognize how listening requires our full attention and presence. Through our efforts to fully engage in the practice of radical listening, we signal a respect for others, which enables us to understand more fully what motivates different framework rationales for actions or interactive choices.

One of the ways socially just ELA teachers signal respect as listeners is by carefully attending to our discourse of listening. We communicate our listening through language and non-verbal actions. As we listen, we can carefully attend to the meaning of the words and messages the speakers communicate. In turn, we gesture as we listen to signal our engagement in the messages we're hearing. By attending to what we are communicating through our facial expressions, hand movements, and posture, we show speakers how invested we are in what they are saying. When we reply, we can carefully attend to the tone of our responses to ensure that we communicate an openness to what the speaker is saying and how they are saying it.

In Natalie's case we saw how carefully she was considering her discourse of listening both in the moment and later as she reflected on her interactions with Max. She wanted to be careful to open space for Max to share candidly and feel heard, even as she sought to encourage him to "be open to thinking about something." She quickly clarified in her reply to Max that being open to consider alternative perspectives "doesn't mean you approve" of that perspective or that you must agree with it. Rather, Natalie understood a need to seek clarity about where Max was coming from in order to gauge where there might be opportunities for further conversation and inquiry. Although Natalie wasn't fully confident in her discourse of listening at the time, we see her investment in reflecting on what her discursive choices afforded her and Max as well as opportunities for continued adjustment.

Discursive listening choices such as those Natalie began to refine are critical tools for helping us zoom in on the ideas and understandings of the students, mentors, colleagues, families, and school leadership with whom we work. Figure 6.1 offers some concrete discursive tools that can serve as invitations for strengthening and expanding your radical listening in the classroom and school communities where you are working and learning.

As with many social processes, the discursive tools in Figure 6.1 support one another. They aren't intended as a recipe card. Rather, they are a set of related discursive practices that many teachers use and overlap as they read interactions and seek to respond to the people and contexts where they engage in these interactions—whether in classrooms, teacher workrooms, hallways, professional development, or the like. What's great about them is that because we engage in social interactions with others every day, we can try them out and reflect on their utility even before entering the space of our clinical classroom and interactions.

As I've shared them with others and worked to hone them in my own practice, I realize that these strategies help me become better attuned to how I message to others that I care about their ideas and them as people. As we develop and perpetually work to strengthen our use of these discursive tools, we become more skilled at reading and responding to sticking points, because we can responsively probe for greater understanding about where people are coming from as well as the frameworks that motivate their engagement with us and with the learning we share.

Tool	Goal	Possibilities for trying it on
Remain present	Demonstrate to the speaker(s) that you're fully invested in listening to what they are saying, undistracted by other things that might simultaneously contend for your attention	• Enter the listening space by recommitting to your goal for attending to speakers' ideas; Why do you want to be fully present? What do you hope to understand? • Remove the temptation of external physical (e.g., cell phones) and mental (e.g., to-do lists) distractions by choosing to actively engage as you listen and concertedly refocus, if you find yourself attending elsewhere; try ○ Notetaking and making as you listen, which, when you record these things in writing, signals to speakers that you're seeking to carefully attend to their ideas; pay particular attention to speakers' frameworks as evidenced in their ideas and actions ○ Summarizing in your head what you understand to be the big ideas that speakers are sharing, which will help you hold on to those ideas ○ Drafting inquiry questions for later follow-up, if you have wonderings that would help you clarify the speaker's intended message or ideas, rather than respond or react
Engage authentically	Use culturally sensitive nonverbals to message to the speaker(s) that you are eager to listen to their ideas	• Read the classroom or speaker nonverbals to gain a better understanding of how people signal their focus and investment in that context. Parrot these nonverbals in your own engagement as a listener. (For example, in many classroom and school communities, turning to face the speaker can singal greater investment in what the speaker is saying. Nodding your head can indicate that you're tracking what the speaker is saying. Sitting, when appropriate, to meet the speaker at the same level can signal that you wish to defer to their ideas as a careful listener.) • Brainstorm with a field instructor or other trusted mentor who has shared knowledge of the same context the kinds of nonverval responses that will signal and be read positively by speakers in the particular classroom or school community where you're working and learning.
Practice silence	Create openings for others to talk before you interject, especially those who might have been or are being subjugated or silenced	• Silence can feel awkward to many but pausing before jumping in to fill a void in talk signals to speakers that you are interested first and foremost in listening to their ideas more than your own.

Figure 6.1 Radical listening discursive tools *(Continued)*

	by systems of inequity, even within schools	• Here, too, notetaking and making can provide you with something to do so that you don't feel as urgently propelled to fill the silence.

Solicit understanding	Express your eagerness to learn from speakers about their needs, interests, goals, and motivations by seeking clarity about what they share with you	• Ask questions about what you have seen or heard the speaker share, especially questions focused on clarifying your understanding of their message and ideas
		• Examples of how to frame such questions:
		  ° "I think I heard you say ___. Am I understanding you accurately?"
		  ° "It seems like ___ is really important to you. Am I following correctly?"
		  ° "Can you say more about ___? I'm eager to learn more/understand."
		  ° "When you said, ___, can you say more about what you mean by that/how that plays out for you?"
		  ° "I'd love to learn more about what meant by ___. Would you be willing to share more about that?"
		  ° "You talked about ___, which seems really important. I'd appreciate knowing more about why that's important in your mind/to your thinking/learning/teaching?"
		  ° "Would you be willing to share more about what led you to (say/do/try ___)?"

Figure 6.1 *(Continued)*

☑ 6.6 Apply your understanding

Try out some of the radical listening strategies in Figure 6.1 or those you've seen others use effectively. You might experiment with them in your everyday life with friends, loved ones, and family. Or you might use them in your clinical work with students, mentors, field instructors, and colleagues. As you do, note the responses you receive from others. What do these moves make possible (or not)? How do people respond? How do you find yourself refining your use of them over time and with practice?

To extend our understanding, let's take a closer look for these practices in another case. As you read on, see if you find evidence of how the candidate in the next case employs radical listening practices as she works to read and understand a sticking point that emerged in her clinical work.

Amelie: A Case Study

Where Natalie's sticking point focused on her interactions with a student, work with mentor teachers and colleagues can also pose sticking points that benefit from efforts to listen carefully.

Amelie was student teaching in a multicultural, multilingual urban classroom. Her mentor teacher had been teaching in the school and district for some time. Pretty early on Amelie realized that her mentor teacher's framework for teaching ELA diverged from her own. Her mentor taught in what Amelie considered to be "traditional, banking" ways. Each unit of study was anchored in the teaching of a canonical text. As they worked through the reading of the text, the mentor paused to ask questions and solicit responses. Formative assessment consisted of multiple-choice reading comprehension tests. Unit summative assessments were academic writing prompts that assessed students' ability to recall the class discussions about the text (Wiggins & McTighe, 2005).

In the first unit of study that Amelie taught which was focused on *Catcher in the Rye* (Salinger, 1991/1951), she explained how her mentor said, "Draw on all my resources for teaching the text as you design your unit." For Amelie, who cares deeply about language, her mentor's choice to encourage her to use "all *my* resources" for "*your* unit," posed a real sticking point. In Amelie's mind, these language choices signaled that the *Catcher* unit would not be hers to design. Instead, she felt her mentor was asking her to replicate the unit and instructional approaches that her mentor employed. This realization felt like a gut punch at the start of her time in her mentor's classroom. She questioned where she might find, even small, entrances to enact some of the socially just approaches that she was so committed to pursuing.

The challenging part was figuring out how to move forward without compromising her relationship with her mentor teacher. Amelie believed that maintaining her ability to work cordially and professionally with her mentor hinged on her ability to not discount or exclude her insights as she weighed how to proceed. As a guest in her mentor teacher's classroom, Amelie believed that her choices about how to respond to this sticking point held important implications for how students viewed her mentor teacher in the immediate and in the five months of the school year that would remain after the conclusion of Amelie's time in the classroom. At the same time, she didn't want to compromise her framework commitment to socially just ELA instruction.

As she brainstormed possibilities for staying as true as possible to her mentor's instructional structures while weaving in some of her own thinking, she scratched off each possibility even before proposing it to her mentor teacher, because she was sure it would either not fly or because it might cause a real riff between them. Finally, Amelie landed on one possibility for focusing the unit on a set of essential questions that analyzed the text's representation of youth. After rehearsing how she would propose the unit framing, Amelie spoke with her mentor teacher. The conversation went as Amelie had feared. Her mentor teacher was not on board. Her mentor teacher encouraged Amelie to use her discussion questions and summative assessment, which she handed to Amelie in an overstuffed manila folder.

Amelie was frustrated. Teaching the unit as her mentor teacher always had felt like giving up entirely on her framework for socially just ELA instruction and, more importantly, she later reflected with colleagues, selling students "short of what they were capable of doing, thinking, and becoming."

She reported having to work "really hard to keep it together" during the conversation with her mentor teacher. In a professional way but also in exasperation, Amelie wondered aloud, "What do you think are your main goals for this unit? What do you really hope students walk away with?" She listened as her mentor repeated comprehension plot lines and thematic ideas that perpetuated critical perspectives "of the text from another era," Amelie shared with colleagues. Not knowing where else to turn, Amelie asked, "What do you think you worry most about me teaching this unit?"

Amelie listened as her mentor shared stories of former colleagues who had been admonished for "going against the curriculum" and bringing up "anything political." What Amelie came to realize is that her mentor teacher was trying to help her "stay neutral."

For Amelie, however, there is no such thing as "neutrality" when it comes to teaching. "Every decision we make as teachers requires us to stake a claim, to take a stand, about what we're teaching and why," she shared with her field instructor and colleagues.[1] Aware that she was teaching during a hotly contested and polarizing election season, she continued.

☞ 6.7 Amelie, in her own words

I think what she means is that I shouldn't touch on subjects that are specifically Democratic or Republican, but that gets tricky you know, because I have students who have family members who are undocumented. I have students who are worried that their families who just immigrated here are going to get deported. If I care about students, I have to talk about the issues that matter to them.

Her mentor teacher advised, instead, saying things like, "Well, that's a good thing to talk about with your parents or in history class." Amelie shared that her mentor's parting words were an encouragement to "just teach the book."

Listening didn't open some magical door to the possibilities Amelie longed to try out with the unit. It did, however, help Amelie understand more about her mentor teacher's framework, and, therefore, about her decision making and hesitancy in allowing Amelie to take some instructional risks. In part, Amelie could more empathetically appreciate that her mentor was trying to protect them both from parental and administrative pushback. She came to appreciate that her mentor teacher wasn't entirely blind to the fact that there were other possibilities for the teaching of the text:

☞ **6.8 Amelie, in her own words**

I think she really doesn't know how to work within the system. Her hands feel tied, and so she's agreed to teach in the only way that gives the appearance of neutrality and safety. I understand that her job is on the line, and there's nothing I want to do to jeopardize that. It's just so tough, because I see these students are eager to engage more fully in conversations that matter to them and their lives, to see how even these canonical texts can inform their today.

Listening helped Amelie rethink her approach and calibrate how best to work with her mentor teacher within this school. Instead, she proposed a one-day trial lesson early in the unit where she could ask students to engage differently with the idea of youth as a social construct. She thought carefully about how to own the potential failure of the idea if it didn't work for her students or her mentor teacher. She asked permission by framing it as an experiment. "I know this might fail, but I'm wondering if I might try just one-day with this idea. Then, I can weave it really well into the next day's lesson," which was her mentor's lesson on the historical background of the text and author. To her surprise, her mentor teacher approved the "experiment." She was more willing to listen, because Amelie was able to frame the idea in relation to the mentor's unit structure and plan, which she would be responsible for running.

We'll return to Amelie's efforts in a later chapter, but for now, let's pause to consider how Amelie's ability and willingness to listen and pose questions improved her understanding of where her mentor was coming from. This understanding led to a less frustrating outcome for Amelie. Yes, she got the opportunity to try out a lesson idea. Perhaps, equally importantly, though, Amelie was able to recalibrate what was and wasn't possible in this classroom context. If she had not been able to listen or solicit conversation that would enable her to hear where her mentor teacher was coming from, she might have set herself up for perpetual head banging and frustration. Sure, Amelie would later make very different choices about how to organize and design instruction in her own classroom. But understanding where her mentor teacher was coming from helped her recalibrate what would be possible and why within the space of her mentor's classroom. It helped her see and then come to terms with the parameters within which she was working more quickly, which helped her ease into the work and maintain a clearer sense of what she was doing and why, which helped her feel more in control of her actions within her mentor's framework rather than her own. This awareness enabled her to distance herself, at times, from the instruction she was delivering while also keeping an eye on what she intended for her future instruction when she had greater independence.

The cases of Kevin, Natalie, and Amelie in this chapter highlight the power of radical listening as an important skillset for delving deeper into our sticking point inquiry. Each of these teachers' exercise of extra caution and efforts to navigate forms of resistance is not unique to their position as pre-service teachers. These are realities and interpersonal dynamics that most veteran teachers face, too, especially if they take the long view and see how everyday choices influence their ability to enact and affect change over time. The discursive tools of radical listening enable us to unearth the layers of complexity that influence our understanding of the sticking points we encounter as we work with others in classroom communities to enact socially just ELA instruction every day, even as we do so with a view toward the future. As Amelie's case made clear and as we'll see in the next chapter, attending to the discourse of our listening aids in our ability to process sticking points so that we can make decisions about how best to respond.

Note

1 Amelie found a helpful distinction between what literacy scholar Hillary Janks (2010, 2012) refers to as little p politics, "the micro- of everyday life. . . the minute-by-minute choices and decisions that make us who we are" and big p Politics (notably capitalized), which is "about government" and other global organizations. Because people are most familiar with Politics, they are often vigilant about considering its influence. However, there is less attention to how politics

are also political. Here Janks draws on "the feminist perspective that the personal *is* political" (2012, p. 151). Little p politics also have a strong influencing power over our everyday interactions, and therefore, teaching and sticking points. Janks suggests that politics and Politics, as social constructs, do act in relationship to one another. For Amelie, however, considering the influencing nature of little p politics on her teaching led her to conclude that her teaching could never be entirely neutral.

References

Adler, D. (2018). Molly's lips. In S. Mitchell (Ed.), *All out: The no-longer-secret stories of queer teens throughout the ages*. Harlequin Teen.

Janks, H. (2010). *Literacy and power*. Routledge.

Janks, H. (2012). The importance of critical literacy. *English Teaching: Practice & Critique, 11*(1), 150–163.

Salinger, J. D. (1991/1951). *The catcher in the rye*. Little, Brown and Co.

Wiggins, G., & McTighe, J. (2005). Thinking like an assessor. In *Understanding by design* (pp. 162–160). ASCD.

7
Taking Stock & Naming: Clarifying New Understandings

Even with the advancement of Global Positioning Satellites (GPS) in our cars and on our phones, there may have literally or metaphorically been times when you've found yourself geographically confused. You may have thought or trusted that you knew where you were going, but finding yourself at an unknown intersection, dead end, neighborhood, or random farm field may have called your assuredness into question. You likely had to pause and take stock of where you really were. You may even have had to retrace your steps to see if you could figure out how you had arrived at this unknown place.

DOI: 10.4324/9781003134442-9

In teaching as in learning, it's not uncommon to find ourselves in uncharted and unknown territory. We journey along feeling confident that we're successfully making sense of what's happening and where we're headed only to find ourselves confused and disoriented. Sticking points, as we've seen, can present moments of disorientation, but so too can our efforts to negotiate them. In these moments we do well to pause and take stock of where we are, including what we know and what we've learned, to reassess where we're headed next.

Seeing What You've Heard and Learned

Let's return briefly to the cases from Chapter Six to consider how listening creates an invitation to take stock of what we've learned through our efforts to zoom in on sticking points through inquiry and radical listening.

If Natalie had not paused to listen longer to Max, she would have missed an opportunity to understand that Max's homophobic comments reflected his limited exposure to conversation about gender and sexuality as well as to people who identified along the gender and/or LGBTQIA+ spectrum. His comments about "trying to express" himself offered important insight into the fact that he was struggling to enter a conversation that was unfamiliar to him and for which he had limited language. His comments, to Natalie, flagged a different kind of future opportunity for interacting with and responding to Max in the context of the classroom and school community.

Amelie's questions for her mentor teacher allowed her to listen longer to where her mentor was coming from in arguing for her particular approaches to the teaching of Catcher in the Rye (Salinger, 1991/1951). If Amelie had not solicited deeper understanding and listened to her mentor's responses, she would have missed an opportunity to learn that her mentor was worried about Amelie doing or saying something that would risk administrative censure and community backlash, which might jeopardize both of their standings in the school. She also learned about another important layer at play in her mentor's decision-making. Her mentor's framework suggested a focus on approaches to teaching the text which were informed by New Critical literary theory would best serve her goal of "staying neutral." If we take as given that all teachers do the best they can with the knowledge they have and intend no harm, then Amelie's mentor teacher was likely working with the resources at her disposal to design instruction. Her mentor's design efforts fit within her instructional framework and her contextual understandings about what it meant to be an effective English language arts (ELA) teacher within a school building where teachers felt pressure to not make waves or bring unnecessary negative attention by discussing current politicized or hot button issues. Taking stock of what her listening yielded afforded Amelie new understanding of where her mentor was coming from, what motivated her action and interactions, and the frameworks that informed those actions. To be sure, it's not that Amelie felt any differently about her own framework for socially just ELA instruction. It's just that she understood the lay of the land more fully and complexly than she had before.

Pausing to take stock of what they learned through their listening afforded Natalie and Amelie new understandings about the complexity of their sticking points. Pausing to take stock reminds us that sticking points emerge through social interactions. Even when we are the ones doing the noticing and naming, sticking points bubble up through our teaching and learning with other people. Without efforts to seek understanding of where those other people are coming from through listening and ongoing interactions, we miss opportunities to better understand the nature of our own sticking points. Beyond that, we do little to honor and mine the riches that inquiring and listening reveal, if we do not pause to take stock of what we've learned about the frameworks that inform others' decision-making and discursive choices. Without that knowledge, it's tough to act in relation to and with those people—whether students, mentors, colleagues, or others.

Zooming Out

Taking stock enables us to consider new information and understanding gained through our listening and inquiry into sticking points.

There's a classic film from 1977 called Powers of Ten that illuminates this point (Earnes & Earnes, 1977).[1] The film begins with a couple enjoying a picnic on a blanket in a Chicago park. Slowly, the picnic image is magnified by the power of ten. The image itself disappears as other things come into view. As the frame zooms ten times further out again and again viewers see the earth and then the solar system. Eventually, the image appears magnified 100 million light years away as completely black outer space. (See Figure 7.1.)

The film illustrates well the power of magnification in how we view the sticking points in our teaching, too. Initially, our identification of a sticking point is a personal journey. We focus on our own experience of the sticking point, and we bring our own frameworks to bear on what we're seeing. But as we zoom out to consider what we've learned from ongoing interactions

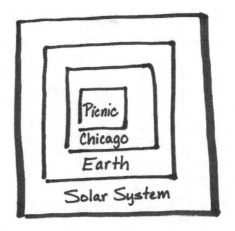

Figure 7.1 Power of Ten zoom out

with others, we are effectively magnifying the sticking point. We begin to see more, understand more, and consider newly what's now more visible, and that includes accounting for others' perspectives and understandings on that same sticking point.

Consider an illustration of how that zooming out process occurred for Natalie in her efforts to negotiate the sticking point with Max in the previous chapter. As Figure 7.2 illustrates, at first, Natalie used her socially just ELA instructional framework to frame the sticking point. Then, she zoomed out to consider what she was learning about Max and his classmates through ongoing interactions with them in the classroom. She zoomed out further to also consider those interactions in relation to what she was learning about the school and local community. This zooming out process enabled Natalie to account not only for continuously evolving interactions, which informed her interpretation of the sticking point, but also for how others' perspectives enabled her to check her own situated perspective. Zooming out, then, supported her ability to take stock of others' frameworks. Knowing that sticking points emerge because of disparate frameworks encourages us to take the time and energy to try and suss out what frameworks inform others' actions and interactive choices—in the case of Natalie, what frameworks were informing Max's comments? Being able to **name** others' frameworks as result of inventorying and assessing what we've learned through inquiry and listening offers a touchpoint for determining next step actions in negotiating sticking points.

Figure 7.2 Natalie's sticking point zoom out

Martha: Case Study

Martha was working in her mentor teacher's classroom on a unit of study in which a canonical text served as the fulcrum, or focal, text (Wessling et al., 2011). With the aid of Martha's careful notetaking, notemaking, and wondering in field notes, she began to see a sticking point emerge as she prepared to teach a lesson within the unit.

☞ 7.1 Martha, in her own words

Typically, my mentor leads discussion using comprehension questions that check for understanding. He'll read aloud a portion of the text, and then pause to ask questions. A student or two responds, and the process repeats again. Honestly, my mentor is doing the heavy lifting here. He's the one in charge and driving the focus. Meanwhile, there are a whole lot of students who rarely, if ever, contribute or engage in the discussion.

In her coursework, Martha recalled learning about this approach to discussion as recitation. Teachers who rely on recitation initiate questions, solicit responses, and evaluate student responses (IRE) to questions that often include known answers (Juzwik et al., 2013). In her notemaking, she commented:

 7.2 Martha, in her own words

I didn't realize until I saw my mentor teacher teaching in the same way I was taught that there is a real need for change in the way teachers teach. I think I had always associated this to different styles of teaching, but now I'm seeing that it is more than that.

The incongruence flagged a sticking point.

As Martha reflected on this sticking point and what she had learned from ongoing classroom inquiry and listening, she named the differences between the frameworks at play in her efforts to consider the role of classroom discussion in her mentor's teaching and in her own. At first Martha called these differences "styles" in her field log entries. But then, she realized that although her mentor teacher said he valued discussion, his framework for discussion differed from her own. He operated from an "IRE framework" that supported "banking education." Martha believed that socially just ELA instruction invites a different framework rationale for the facilitation of discussion. In her estimation, socially just ELA instruction cultivates "dialogic approaches to teaching students how to engage in discussion." It centers disciplinary inquiry around problem-posing and the exploration of textual puzzles that position students as knowledge-producers (Rainey, 2017). Martha's earliest noticings and wonderings began to coalesce around a set of questions:

 7.3 Martha, in her own words

How does modeling relate to socially just teaching? How do we know when it is appropriate to model versus lecture versus have students do it on their own?

Martha's questions suggest a desire to scaffold students' learning to talk so that they can independently and dialogically contribute to the academic talk in her ELA classroom—and ultimately, beyond. She believes that it is her role to model for students how to engage in effective, dialogic discussion.

The ability to distill and then name these two frameworks for herself enabled Martha to see how, because her mentor teacher's framework differed from her own, they were differently motivated to include more student voices in the discussion. For her teacher, the involvement of students in discussion served his ability to evaluate their responses. For Martha, the goal of diverse student involvement in the discussion was multifold. First, Martha explained her belief that student engagement increases when students believe their lived experiences matter in class discussion:

☞ **7.4 Martha, in her own words**

If you give students a chance to discuss what they go through in their personal lives, you will get a more thoughtful, student-led, conversation.

At the same time, she believed that student perspectives needed to be carefully affirmed and at times challenged. Aware that the fulcrum canonical text prioritized the experiences of white protagonists, Martha was eager to infuse more inquiry-driven discussions about the text in conjunction with counternarratives that decentered white lived experience and invited students to apply critical theoretical perspectives, which would make visible nondominant lived experiences, especially in a predominantly white classroom (Baker-Bell, 2020; Borsheim-Black & Sarigianides, 2019; Haviland, 2008; Tanner, 2019). She reflected,

☞ **7.5 Martha, in her own words**

I plan to encourage multiple perspectives and interpretations in my journey as an ELA teacher because I believe it is an ethical obligation as a socially just educator to have open conversations with my students as a way to not only invite multiple perspectives but to encourage students to open their perspectives up to those around them to help navigate this world together and develop holistic perspectives.

If, as Martha's framework supported and she reflected, learning is socially constructed, textual analysis and interpretation is best served by multiple voices and perspectives as well as chances to reflect on and strengthen one's ability to situate perspectives in relation to others.

Martha's ability to name the two frameworks, IRE and dialogic instruction, that bubbled up during her observations and listening provided her with a way of quickly capturing and holding on to the different approaches she described in her field log notemaking and wondering. The act of naming provided clarity in understanding the nature of the sticking point she was experiencing as she observed and supported her mentor teacher's teaching while preparing to teach her own lesson in that classroom. We'll return to Martha in a later chapter to discuss how this naming supported her ability to negotiate and act in response to the sticking point.

How do we Name Frameworks?

What matters most for the purposes of this chapter is that Martha *named* and distinguished the two frameworks that resulted in a sticking point for her. Naming frameworks affords us opportunity to zoom out and reflect on the nature of the sticking points we face in our teaching. The ability to name frameworks enables us to describe important differences in frameworks. In short, naming shapes and reflects how we process sticking points, especially in relation to our socially just ELA framework for teaching and learning.

Naming frameworks is a lot like the process that people use to name their playlists. We decide how to capture the essence of a group of songs such that it reflects our analysis of their common characteristics. How we title a playlist enables us to quickly find, sort, and play music. Our naming system must only make sense to us, since we are the ones who want to be able to easily access our music. The names we choose help us take stock of what is present in our musical libraries so that we can decide what to do next. If we endeavor to make sense of a friend or loved one's playlist, we seek to figure out their rationale and naming conventions only in as much as it helps us understand their organizing principles. We don't have to agree with their choices in music or naming. We just seek to understand it so that we can make sense of their thinking and, in turn, playlist.

In Chapter Two, we learned about how teaching always includes overlapping and interacting frameworks—both our own and others' frameworks. Like playlist naming processes, being able to name frameworks when sticking points emerge enables us to quickly capture the essence of each framework and categorize it in relation to other frameworks. Naming frameworks helps us reflect on where, if at all, these frameworks overlap or intersect. Where frameworks do not relate well to one another, where there are clear sticking points, being able to name frameworks distinctly allows us to quickly

• course readings or conversations • professional readings or research	• other people's names or language • a brief description of the framework's primary rationale for action or goal	• your questions or field log language about observations

Figure 7.3 Naming framework sources

describe the essence of each framework before determining what action, if any, we wish to take.

Notably, the process of naming is personal. Our naming helps us reflect individually on which frameworks are at play in the sticking points that emerge in our teaching. Without being able to describe, or name, what's at play, we cannot fully determine how best to respond and, importantly, whether and when to involve others in that negotiation process.

To be sure, as Martha's case illustrates, by naming frameworks using keywords and phrases, or tags, which make the most sense to us personally, it's likely that we'll be drawing on our learning in coursework and the field. Martha drew heavily on her evolving framework understandings about socially just ELA instruction and its overlapping relationship to dialogic teaching. These are terms and phrases that she had picked up in coursework readings and conversations, which she honed in fieldwork conversations with field instructors and other mentor teachers, and vice versa. Like playlist naming, Martha's naming evolved organically through her field log notetaking, note-making, and wonderings where she worked to first notice and then reflect on emerging differences in what she saw her mentor teacher doing and what she aspired to achieve through her facilitation of discussion.

Figure 7.3 offers a short list of sources from which to draw as we name for ourselves frameworks at work in the sticking points we encounter as teachers. This list is not meant to be exhaustive. Rather, it's meant to get you started. Feel encouraged to add to the list as you take note of the process you develop for naming frameworks across time.

☑ 7.6 Apply your understanding

To practice naming frameworks, examine the curricular materials or pedagogical texts available to you in your field classroom or school, or university or college library. As you review the table of contents, chapters, sample activities, assignments, assessments, or lesson ideas, name for yourself the framework approach(es) you see to ELA instruction.

Consider the kinds of overarching rationales or motivating goals for instruction that are apparent to you in your review of these materials. How would you name these rationales or goals? If possible, share your thinking with a colleague or mentor. The goal of sharing isn't to assess whether you share a name for the framework(s) but rather to rehearse and reflect on your process for naming as a way of strengthening and clarifying your skillful naming of frameworks.

Darby: Case Study

While Martha's sticking point involved her mentor teacher's framework, Darby's sticking point emerged during a characterization lesson in her interaction with a student, Dedrick. Similarly, though, Darby's efforts to solicit understanding about Dedrick's framework by listening and inquiring opened space for her to take stock of what motivated Dedrick's concern about grades. Early in the lesson, Darby modeled how readers begin to track character development across a novel. During her modeling, Dedrick raises his hand.

[3:07-3:47]

DEDRICK: Do I have to know everything about her character to get a really good grade?

DARBY: I wouldn't focus on the grade in this aspect. I would focus on understanding how her character is developed throughout the text. In the future, we're going to be talking about a lot of characters. This character map isn't meant to quiz you or trick you to think, 'Oh, I need to know this character trait about this character,' but rather how those character traits impact how they are as people.

DEDRICK: So, there won't be a quiz on this then?

DARBY: No, there will not. No. This is about developing your understanding of a character, because that will influence your reading of a book.

DEDRICK: [nods in agreement]

A few minutes later, Dedrick raises another version of the same grading question:

[6:50 – 7:37]

DARBY: ... right, so this helps us see how choosing a quote from the text can be indicative of

DEDRICK: [raises hand]

DARBY: the character in the novel. Yes, Dedrick?

DEDRICK: So, if I write down this stuff [pointing to what Darby has written on the board], can I get an "A" on this worksheet?

DARBY: Again, I don't want you to think about this in terms of grading but in terms of holistically understanding a character. Because, if you think about it, when you're trying to get to know a person in real life, you don't try to memorize things about them so that you can pin them down to a tee but rather so that you can understand them. So, this process and us going over it in class is for us to develop an understanding of the character that's more than, 'Oh, I know this character because she is [gestures a line with her hands] blank,' but rather that might help us get a glimpse into one aspect of who she is as a character.

In these exchanges, it's clear Darby tries to shift Dedrick's attention away from his fixation on how everything is directly related to the grades he'll ultimately earn in the class and toward an understanding of why what they're doing will help the class grow as readers of texts.

Nonetheless, as Darby reflected on the lesson, she was keenly aware of how she might need to help Dedrick develop this understanding across time. Darby empathized with Dedrick's anxiety about earning an "A" grade as she sought to strategize a way forward in her ability to work with Dedrick.

☞ 7.7 **Darby, in her own words**

I know that in most classes, everything's driven by points. Dedrick has lived in so many classrooms where the main goal is to earn as many points as possible. The goal is points, not understanding, not growth as readers and writers. It's no wonder that he finds it frustrating when I don't feed into that same framework.

Darby, whose framework for assessment aligned well with her mentor teacher's framework, was much more interested in helping students see the rationale for why their learning mattered, including how what they were learning would support their independent ability to draw and revise conclusions about characters as they read the class novel as well as their choice reading. Darby's goals were larger than points:

☞ 7.8 Darby, in her own words

In my teaching, I wish to continue to emphasize that there are various forms to interpret a text. This is something that I have consistently tried to enact in my lesson plans where I made a point to articulate that what I'm modeling is just one of many possible ways of thinking about a text. This was done to not only show students that my way of thinking is just one possibility, but it was also done to empower students to conduct their own thinking and lines of inquiry.

For Darby, promoting students' ability to ultimately "conduct their own thinking and lines of inquiry" through her teaching enabled her to act on her commitment to equitable and just assessment practices, which were connected to a socially just ELA instructional framework. Nonetheless she realized that helping students live and find a different kind of success in a classroom with a different framework than the one they likely had spent more time enculturated into in previous courses would require some negotiation and careful reflection.

In her field log and lesson annotations, Darby posed the following inquiry question: "How do I make sure that students feel heard in the classroom while also ensuring that they do not feel restricted by a certain way of thinking and learning?" As she continued, she referred to Dedrick's framework for assessment and grading as "points-driven" and hers as "holistically focused." To be clear, Darby did not seek to make these distinctions in order to suggest that Dedrick's framework for grading was "wrong" and hers was "right." To the contrary, she wrote:

☞ 7.9 Darby, in her own words

Both Dedrick and I are on some level living in a points-driven system. It's all around us. Just walk down the halls of this school, of any school really. He and I both know that at the end of the day, I will have to assign a grade that reflects his ability to enact the lesson and unit objectives. But I think we can learn to live together within that system and still work toward a larger more holistic vision of what we can accomplish together. I wish to disrupt the traditional model of assessment and grading as "banking" where teachers are the all-knowing voices that "fill" students with information and assess based on students' ability to regurgitate that information. I truly believe that teachers should learn from students just as much as students learn from teachers and that the two parties should work together as meaning-makers in the classroom. To do this, I wish to build my classroom around student inquiry and to empower students to take an active role in their education. I want my assessment feedback to help students grow toward that goal rather than fulfill a points system framework.

For Darby, distinguishing a "points-driven" from a "holistic" framework enabled her to understand the nature of her sticking point.

Darby's ability to take stock and zoom out helped her to see how her sticking point didn't have to do with Dedrick so much as it was about the system that Dedrick had become so familiar with as *the* rationale for assessment. Understanding these distinctions enabled Darby to reflect on the frameworks at work, and, therefore, at stake, for both Dedrick and her in their learning together. And, as we'll explore in the next chapter, these understandings helped her reframe the nature of the sticking point so that she could make a more strategic decision about how to respond.

Systems Considerations

As Darby's experience highlights, too, there's value in making sure that our efforts to zoom out consider the systems we're working within and, at times, against. As socially just ELA instructors, we recognize that we work within systems of inequity and that those systems of inequity have historically and continue to foreclose opportunities for learning and access to high-quality instruction for students from marginalized and minoritized populations. Enacting socially just instruction requires an awareness of the constraints of the systems we're working within as well as savviness in identifying places where we can work differently or push against the normative ways in which that system operates without risking our ability to continue to work within that system. The balance is a tricky one, but recognizing the ways these systems are at work in our day-to-day professional interactions can help us interpret and, ultimately, as we'll explore in the next chapter, reframe our understanding of the sticking points we face. In Darby's case, for example, her ability to engage in systems thinking meant that she could situate Dedrick's comments within a system they were both a part of, which enabled her to think differently about what was at stake for both of them and how she might make incremental, slow change over time rather than overnight.

Zooming out to consider systems in our interpretation of sticking points thus requires that we simultaneously entertain what can be done immediately and long-term.

 7.10 Apply your understanding

If you applied your understanding in Chapter Two, Figure 2.7, by re-searching more about the context where you will be or are engaged in fieldwork, revisit your notemaking and inquiry questions. Or, look back at your notetaking, notemaking, and inquiry questioning from a field log you completed in a classroom where you are or have been working. To what extent are your wonderings reflective of your think-ing about how systems, and in particular systems of inequity, influence what you learned through your research? Annotate your thinking to in-dicate where you're considering how systems (e.g., the school district, mandated curriculum, economic) influence the day-to-day classroom interactions you will or have observed. Then, annotate your noticing to practice naming frameworks that your notetaking, notemaking, and inquiry questions reveal about your own or others' frameworks.

 7.11 Reflecting

After you've completed box 7.10, reflect in writing or with others on what you noticed about your own awareness of how systems influence your day-to-day interactions and instruction in a particular classroom context and how your notetaking, notemaking, and inquiry question-ing supports your ability to name frameworks. How is the process help-ing you zoom in to learn more that might help you understand more fully the nature of the sticking points you're noticing? Or is it? What do you need or want to continue to practice? To see? To understand about the process and what it makes visible?

Note

1 You can easily access this film to see how it plays by searching for "Powers of Ten movie" on the web.

References

Baker-Bell, A. (2020). *Linguistic justice: Black language, literacy, identity, and pedagogy.* Routledge.

Borsheim-Black, C., & Sarigianides, S. T. (2019). *Letting go of literary whiteness: Antiracist literature instruction for white students.* Teachers College Record.

Earnes, C., & Earnes, R. (Director). (1977). *Powers of ten.* A film dealing with the relative size of things in the universe and the effect of adding another zero [Film] Pyramid Films.

Haviland, V. (2008). "Things get glossed over": Rearticulating the silencing power of whiteness. *Journal of Teacher Education, 59*(1), 40–54. doi: https://doi.org/10.1177/0022487107310751.

Juzwik, M. M., Borsheim-Black, C., Caughlan, S., & Heintz, A. (2013). *Inspiring dialogue: Talking to learn in the English classroom.* Teachers College Press.

Rainey, E. C. (2017). Disciplinary literacy in English language arts: Exploring the social and problem-based nature of literary reading and reasoning. *Reading Research Quarterly, 52*(1), 53–71. http://www.jstor.org.libproxy.lib.ilstu.edu/stable/26622578

Salinger, J. D. (1991/1951). *The catcher in the rye.* Little, Brown and Co.

Tanner, S. J. (2019). Whiteness is a white problem: Whiteness in English education. *English Education, 51*(2), 182–199.

Wessling, S. B., Lillge, D., & VanKooten, C. (2011). *Supporting students in a time of core standards: Grades 9–12.* National Council of Teachers of English.

8
Reframing Interpretation: Finding Entrances to Action

To this point, we have developed a shared understanding of how a framework for socially just English language arts (ELA) instruction offers a lens for noticing and framing sticking points as we work within field-based classrooms to enact our commitments to teach for justice. We've explored how these sticking points often emerge when we encounter different frameworks that offer seemingly divergent rationales for action. And we've considered how the emergence of sticking points presents us with opportunities to zoom in and learn more before we decide how to respond. Ongoing inquiry and

DOI: 10.4324/9781003134442-10

radical listening can help us get a better sense of the nature of the sticking points we face. By taking stock of what we've learned, we begin to zoom out and name the frameworks at play, which help us account for others' perspectives and rationales for action and which affect our own decisions about how to act in response.

It may justifiably seem that after the patience required to inquire, listen, and take stock, action is the obvious next step. As teachers, we're doers. Most of us are eager to act. As socially just ELA teachers, we're eager to affect change—often because we know how very long real change, the struggle for justice, can take.

Yet, if we jump from naming to action, we will have missed a critical step in the process. That next step, reframing, is the focus of this chapter. Jumping to action without pausing to consider whether and then how to reframe our sticking points would risk disregarding all that we have learned.

Reframing Defined

We know from Chapter Four that framing is about initially interpreting the nature of a sticking point after we notice its emergence. Doing so helps us hang onto the sticking point so that we can explore it further in an effort to deepen our understanding of it. Often, what we've learned will cause us to revisit and reconsider the nature of the sticking point by asking ourselves, "Does what I've learned prompt me to reinterpret what's going on here?"

As ELA teachers, we have intimate experience with the process of reinterpretation through our lives as readers. Consider how as we read texts, we begin to frame what we know and understand about particular characters and the conflicts they face. Early on, we take textual details into consideration to frame the conflicts these characters face. As we read, further information and understanding often invites us to reinterpret interactions between and among characters as well as the nature of the conflicts they face.

In our reading lives, our reinterpretation of the text with the benefit of new information and understanding becomes an active process. It's ongoing and directly responsive to what we're learning and uncovering as we read. In fact, that's part of what we work diligently to help students understand and appreciate. Reinterpretation is part of the joy of reading. Reinterpretation is part of understanding how complex social interactions always beget new understanding and, we hope, empathy about the complexity of the human experience—not only our own, but also of others.

When it comes to sticking points in our teaching lives, remaining open and anticipating the need to continually reinterpret positions us well in our efforts to work most generously and purposefully with others in our classrooms and schools. This process of reinterpretation is **reframing**. More specifically, reframing is the active process whereby we seek to re-see or newly see the sticking points that emerge in our teaching and learning. As the name suggests, reframing is about revisiting and reconsidering our initial interpretation bearing in mind what we've learned and been able to conclude, especially as relates to the various frameworks at play.

Reframing is predicated on an assumption that we have initially framed our sticking points. In Chapter Four, we said that sticking points could easily be misunderstood as roadblocks that prevent action. However, framing suggests differently a way of viewing sticking points as malleable and open to reinterpretation, as resources for supporting our own teaching and ongoing professional learning. As framing's companion, reframing offers us a tool for finding entrances into action, especially where those entrances might otherwise not be easily identified or seen in relation to other people and other frameworks.

Benefits

Let's revisit some cases from previous chapters to see how reframing provided each teacher candidate with a more visible entrance for choosing whether and how to act in response to what they learned about the nature of the sticking points faced.

Natalie: Case Study, Revisited

For Natalie (from Chapter Six), zooming in and out enabled her to reframe the sticking point she faced in her interactions with Max. You'll remember Natalie's sticking point had to do with Max's comments about "trying to express himself" as a cisgender, heterosexual male who found it challenging to apply a gender lens to his reading of a short story with a queer identifying character. Early on, she, like her colleagues, framed Max's comments from a deficit perspective. She focused on whether to correct Max's language. After inquiring and listening, she came to understand differently the root cause of Max's comments. As Natalie took stock of what she had learned, she saw how Max's comments were a byproduct of his framework for classroom talk, which prioritized heteronormative identities and language.

Contextual and Interactional Responsiveness

Our ability to reframe sticking points, as in Natalie's case, benefits from ongoing interactions with others and across time. But it also benefits from understanding that our ongoing interactions with others across time occur in particular contexts (e.g., classrooms, schools, districts, communities, and states) and systems. Deepening our understanding of these contexts also influences our understanding of the sticking points we navigate. Because Natalie sought to inquire about the ways in which community and school norms influenced Max's framework, she understood differently his comments. Figure 8.1 offers a graphic representation of Natalie's journey to reframe her sticking point in light of her learning as she zoomed out.

The result? Natalie reframed the sticking point. She came to see Max's comments as a reflection of his unfamiliarity with language to talk about and be in community with those whose gender and sexual orientation differed from those of his experience and dominant norms. Natalie came to see that Max's efforts to language his unfamiliarity could be reinterpreted as an implicit request and openness to learn, even if not to agree. Reframing offered Natalie new entrance for acknowledging and appreciating Max's candor as well as his desire to explore new ways of being in conversation

Figure 8.1 Natalie's reframing

about identities that differed from his own and from those most frequently prioritized in his community. Her inquiry and listening as well as efforts to take stock opened an opportunity for engaging in different kinds of learning conversations in future interactions with Max and his classmates. She could assume a much less combative and deficit-oriented approach by positioning herself differently.

Embracing the Ability to Rethink and Resee

Natalie expressed a feeling of humility about what she had learned. She genuinely sought ways to remain open and empathetic to her students' identities, perspectives, and questions. It was humbling to learn that had she not engaged in this process of sticking point negotiation, with its requisite need for patience and prioritizing an understanding of others' frameworks, she might have dismissed or missed Max's willingness to share uncertainty and request for help in joining new kinds of conversations—really, to be in different kinds of community with others without feeling pressure to agree. Natalie, like so many teachers committed to teaching for justice, sees this as a central goal of her teaching.

More fundamentally, Natalie offers a reminder that to be effective socially just ELA teachers, we must embrace interactional processes like sticking point negotiation that enable us to continually position ourselves as learners who benefit from the lessons we learn about and from others—our students, colleagues, mentors, and communities. Losing the ability to take stock means we dangerously position ourselves as infallible and expert. That's not to diminish our growing professional knowledge and rhetorical savviness. Rather, it keeps us humble to the fact that negotiating sticking points can help us embrace the evolution of our own understandings—a critical way of enacting and modeling the very thing we hope our instruction will make possible for students.

Amelie: Case Study, Revisited

Amelie (from Chapter Six) reframed her sticking point, which had to do with her mentor's urging to teach a unit of study as she had, in ways that enabled Amelie to see her relationship with her mentor teacher differently. What she learned through her ongoing inquiry and listening helped her resist the initial urge to label her mentor as unwilling to change. Instead, she came to understand more deeply how her mentor's frameworks for ELA teaching emerged from her own lived experiences and interactions within a particular school community and with the teaching of texts there. This understanding helped to explain why her mentor was devoted to her framework rationales for how to teach a canonical text.

Reframing invited Amelie to recalibrate her approach and understand what was and wasn't possible within the classroom context her mentor shared with her. These new understandings, ultimately, led Amelie to appreciate how different things were at stake for her mentor in the decisions they were making about the teaching of the unit. These understandings also enabled Amelie to rethink her own approach to teaching the unit within that class-room context. She realized that asking her mentor for permission to overhaul her teaching of the unit would expand the chasm in their work together, and that chasm could further challenge Amelie's ability to take instruc-tional risks in future instruction. She realized that her mentor had reason to question whether she could trust Amelie's instructional choices. If Amelie continued to dismiss her mentor's ideas, she might never gain her mentor's confidence in her ability to work successfully with her. As a result of this awareness, Amelie rethought her approach. Instead, she decided to see if she could carve out small spaces to experiment with her efforts to enact socially just ELA instruction within her mentor's existing curriculum.

Honoring Complexity as an Act of Justice

As Amelie's case makes clear, reframing isn't always about finding simple, easy entrances that everyone automatically agrees upon. Reframing enables us to gain a more nuanced and balanced perspective on the nature of the sticking points we face. Nuance and perspective come from the ability to zoom in and out to consider the perspectives and frameworks of those with whom we teach and learn.

Moreover, pausing to consider whether reframing is necessary and then how we might reframe in light of what we've learned is an act of justice. Ignoring a sticking point or assuming that our interpretation of that sticking point is surefire positions us in ways that message our unwillingness to carefully con-sider the perspectives and frameworks of others who have much to teach us, even if or especially when they differ from our own. To ignore what we can learn from inquiring, listening, and taking stock could be more injurious and unjust than we intend. The people who we interact with are complex beings, just as are we. The places where we learn and teach are complex systems, often of inequity. Without an effort to understand and work with people and within these systems, we compromise our ability to affect change.

Uncovering Opportunities

When we honor the people who we're working so closely with and in support of by learning from and about their perspectives and frameworks, we uncover new ways to frame our sticking points in relation to them and the systems within which we work. Our efforts to reframe often reveal entrances to new possibilities where there may have otherwise appeared none or which were, before we inquired and listened radically, unavailable. Embracing the negotiation process opens opportunities for action.

Reframing in Action

To see how reframing benefits from the process of zooming in and out in our negotiation of sticking points, let's explore the case of Jess whose sticking point reflected interactions with his mentor and students in his mentor's classroom as well as the department and district.

Jess: Case Study

Jess's classroom was embedded within a racially and economically diverse suburban school. Early on, Jess observed his mentor, Jill, teach and interact with students during independent work time or in small groups to "get to know them and support their learning."

Noticing

Through these earliest interactions, Jess noticed that Jill relied heavily on canonical texts as the centerpieces of units of study. His notetaking included descriptions of classroom conversation where Jill asked comprehension questions about the text. Students responded with short answers. At the end of units, the department's common summative assessments were often literary analyses of the text that the whole class studied together.

Framing

Through his notemaking, Jess logged conversations with Jill where she described one of her professional goals as not "rocking the ship," a reference to maintaining the school system and department's curricular status quo. In Jess's notemaking, he saw this approach as connected to an emergent sticking point: students' lack of engagement in course content. In his interactions with students, Jess felt that students were working to "do what she [Jill] wants." It was clear to Jess that Jill cared about her students, and they were eager to talk with her about their experiences in and out of class. Jess's earliest framing of the sticking point, he felt, was a byproduct of exclusive curricular and instructional focus on canonical texts. This focus, Jess surmised, reflected why students "had trouble relating to what was going on in these texts" and "why literary analysis as a skill set mattered beyond this classroom."

Inquiring

To learn more, Jess asked Jill to read students' summative and formative assessment work. He reviewed the department's common rubric for grading the literary analysis essays and noted what was prioritized and valued. In particular, he was struck by the standardization and efforts to generalize common writing skills that "applied to all writing, rather than those skills that were specific to students' learning and understanding of how to rhetorically respond to their goals as writers, to their understanding of genre, and to write for authentic audiences."

Radical Listening

Jess also set out to delve deeper as he continued to interact with Jill and students. When he worked one-on-one or with small groups of students, he would casually inquire: "How do you think this might help you in the future?" In his field notetaking, he logged their responses, which generally included the following types of comments:

> "I have no idea."
> "I think it will help prepare us for next year. I heard things get harder."
> "I'm probably going to need this stuff for college, I guess."

Listening prompted Jess to see more at play than he had initially seen. As the frequency of students' comments about relevance connected to college increased, Jess began to see that students had bought into Jill's messages about the need to pursue college. Their challenge seemed to be in gaining access to the skills needed for life beyond high school.

At the same time, Jess asked Jill a lot of questions about how she approached her teaching, including where she found opportunities to differentiate instruction or adapt instruction to speak directly to students' lived experiences and previous learning. In his notemaking he commented further.

 8.1 Jess, in his own words

I have the sense that Jill sees adaptation and differentiation as connected almost exclusively to meeting students' Individualized Educational Plans (IEPs). She talks a lot about how this is a non-tracked class. It's difficult to meet the range of learning needs in this class. She shared how "getting everyone ready for college" means that everyone has to end up in the same place. "Some kids just can't get there. It's tough."

Jess also wondered about the system wide support teachers in the district were receiving for "expanding their understanding about how differentiation and adaptation of instruction benefit all learners, including those who need and deserve challenges and curricula that reflects who they are and who they need to understand in an increasingly globalized world."

Taking Stock

Jess's inquiry and listening revealed multi-layered understandings about the nature of students' lack of engagement. For Jess, Jill's decision-making was, at least in part, influenced by the system she was working within as well as her access to and solicitation of ongoing opportunities to learn about and strengthen her understanding of how to "meet a range of learners" in her classes. Jess saw the limits of a common assessment and the department's expectation that all teachers meet the same "learning targets using the same methods." This, in Jess's estimation, presented ELA teachers in the department with some "very real barriers to their autonomy to tailor instruction and assessment while still meeting required standards." At the same time, Jess was keenly aware of students' struggles to understand the relevance of what they were learning and doing in class not just for future coursework but, importantly for Jess, beyond classroom walls. Jess wrote in his notemaking:

8.2 Jess, in his own words

There's little effort to teach for transfer or to meet the strengths and needs of individual learners. A one-size fits all approach is an injustice to all students' learning and ability to see themselves as capable learners and contributors.

Naming

Jess came to see that understanding his "student engagement sticking point" required naming a set of frameworks that reflected Jill's instructional goals and student understanding of the purposes of ELA learning. Jill's framework for teaching ELA, Jess concluded, prioritized "career and college readiness." The framework aligned with or may have resulted from the department's focus on this aspect of ELA teaching and learning, which they saw as directly responsive to the Common Core State Standards (Common Core State Standards Initiative, 2021). Many students, Jess noticed, began to adopt similar language about the relevance of their learning as connected to college preparation, less so about career. (In fact, in his notetaking, Jess started to track the emphasis on college over career, too.) For many students, Jess concluded, the reason for doing the work of the ELA class was "to get ready for college." But there were other students who struggled to articulate any rationale for what they were learning and why, and this troubled Jess just as much.

Reframing

As Jess reflected on his initial framing of the sticking point, he shared, "I was frustrated when I didn't see in-roads around all kinds of sticking points, including students' lack of engagement in the course content." Jess was concerned that Jill's chosen methods and the department's constant push to create relevance through comments about how students would need to learn the skills "to be successful in college" alienated students who struggled to see themselves as college "material" or for whom college did not seem a financial possibility. Jess came to reframe the sticking point. Instead of focusing on "the catch-all student engagement, as if it's students' fault that they're not engaged," he continued,

8.3 Jess, in his own words

I think the sticking point has more to do with limited instructional modeling that enables students to really gain an understanding of what it looks like to take up and rehearse the literacy skills they'll need in their future career and college pathways. But I also think that modeling would help them appreciate how literacy skills and understandings can enrich their lives and deepen their appreciation of what we gain when we study language. So, yes, it's about college and career readiness, but it's about so much more. How will students be able to appreciate that unless they truly see it in action in class and in life beyond?

Without this reframing, Jess may well have missed a chance to identify modeling as an opening to both enact his commitment to a socially just ELA framework within Jill's classrooms *and* align his efforts with Jill's framework commitment to college and career readiness. For Jess, negotiating this sticking point led to an important opportunity to develop a stronger connection in his own pedagogical knowledge about the link between modeling and socially just ELA:

 8.4 Jess, in his own words

I'm coming to see modeling is extremely important to socially just ELA instruction, because it focuses the lesson, my teaching, on helping students learn the skills of reading and writing rather than memorizing content or, worse yet, blindly trying to figure out what to do. I'm working to model skills in ways that help students see how what we're learning transfers to their lives and helps them contribute to important social change in their relationships, lives, and communities.

Conclusion

In our professional lives, others often frame the work of ELA teaching for us. We receive curriculum guides, which someone has framed in particular ways to emphasize certain content, skills, texts, and goals. We are beholden to standards that frame ELA for specific purposes by virtue of what understandings, skills, and purposes are prioritized. We are informed of district or school policies and initiatives through documents and communication that frame them to accomplish or uphold certain visions and frameworks for teaching and learning. In short, things will always be framed for us. We get to choose whether and then how to reframe them to align with our commitment to socially just ELA instruction. Or we may choose to reframe them to make visible for others how they are inconsistent with a commitment to teaching for justice. Or we may reframe them in our classrooms to help students see how our obligation to fulfill what we've been given or what's been outlined can serve the larger goals we've developed and fostered that articulate rationales consistent with our frameworks and research in support of socially just ELA instruction. Reframing offers us a powerful reminder of our own agency and power to shape and reshape the narrative. How, when, and why we choose to reframe offers us space to see how, even in spaces where it may seem we're confined and obliged to fulfill what's been dictated to us, we have opportunities to make decisions about how we respond in ways that are consistent with our larger goal of teaching ELA as an act of and in support of social justice.

☑ 8.5 Apply your understanding

As you reflect on the cases in Part II and the sticking points that have emerged through your interactions in classrooms and the systems that shape those interactions, consider the evolution of your own thinking about the nature of those sticking points. How has your engagement in the process of negotiation helped you see possibilities for action? Pick a sticking point that you've noticed or that has emerged for you in your field-based interactions. Then, just as you read about in this chapter with Jess's case, describe for yourself or share with others how the negotiation process has helped you evolve your own understanding of that sticking point.

Notice – Using your notetaking and notemaking, how did the sticking point emerge? Provide specifics about instances and interactions.

Frame – How did you initially interpret what was going on with this sticking point?

Inquire – What inquiry question(s) did you pursue through further observation, interaction, radical listening, and study in the space?

Listen Radically – What did your listening help you understand?

Take Stock – As you zoom out and reflect, what did you learn through your inquiry?

What did you learn about or from people?

What did you learn about or from the systems that influence and affect what and where you're teaching?

Name – How in your own words, would you name the frameworks at play in this sticking point?

Reframe – In light of the above reflections, how, if at all, might you reinterpret the sticking point?

Strategize Action – Keeping in mind the individual and systems considerations at play here, what possibilities for strategically responding to this sticking point might exist?

 8.6 Reflecting

After you've completed box 8.5, reflect in writing or talk with others to explore how describing your negotiation process helped you evolve your understanding of the sticking point. How has it revealed different possibilities for action that might not otherwise have been visible or available to you at first? What has it helped you understand about sticking points and your ability or understanding about to negotiate them, especially within the context of the particular classroom or interaction you're navigating?

Reference

Common Core State Standards Initiative. (2021). English Language Arts Standards. http://www.corestandards.org/ELA-Literacy/

Part III
Moving Forward

Teaching, like life, is cyclical. Semesters and school years technically end. Students move on to the next grade. They graduate. But our teaching lives chug on. Knowing that sticking points will continue to bubble up in our teaching and professional interactions can be unsettling for those without a concrete process for negotiation. In Part III, we'll consider how embracing the negotiation process is a gift we give ourselves: a means of navigating future sticking points, even if we can't anticipate what exactly they'll look like or when they'll emerge.

It's a particular kind of gift. I invite you to resist a precarious assumption that what we're learning from our own and others' stories of sticking point negotiation is how to hit the repeat button with the goal of making similar decisions. As we've explored throughout this book, sticking points are interactionally driven. Because our interactions happen within specific classroom and school cultures, we don't want to presume that what works for one teacher working within one classroom or school will necessarily play out similarly for us or even that what worked yesterday or last semester will serve those we teach equally well now. Instead, in Part III, we'll revisit why what

DOI: 10.4324/9781003134442-11

we want to take away from our learning through others' stories, or cases, is the value of embracing the negotiation process. The process is what's replicable, less the outcomes. Engaging the process is what will help us discern the best course or courses of action in-the-moment and in the future.

To further solidify our understanding of the utility of this process in the stories we're writing through our own teaching and professional growth, in Part III we'll also meet veteran teachers who have come to see the negotiation process as central to their ability to enact socially just instruction in their classrooms, professional learning communities, schools, and districts. In fact, they have come to see how engaging this process not only enables them to respond to sticking points with care for those they work and learn with, where they teach and learn, it also sustains and renews their commitment to teaching ELA for justice across time.

9
Taking Action

English language arts (ELA) teachers understand the power of story. We like to contemplate what stories reveal to us about human experience and how we benefit from reading the stories of others whose lived experiences may differ from our own. Some of us even admit to reading ahead so that we know the resolution of a story from the start before we return to earlier chapters to learn how the characters arrive at the end.

In Part II, you may well have wondered as you read through cases, "What did each teacher ultimately decide to do?" I hope that the logic for delaying these endings will become clearer as we consider how the process for negotiating sticking points sets in motion our ability to take action in response.

Cases, Revisited

Let's revisit the cases you've read about thus far. Figure 9.1 summarizes the action that the teachers in each case took after engaging in the negotiation process. You'll notice that action takes many forms, including but not limited to shifts

DOI: 10.4324/9781003134442-12

Chapter	Teacher	Reframed Sticking Point	Action
1	Alex	Students did not choose the "socially just" reading assessment options	Revised reading assessment options for future iterations of the assignment
2	Cruz	Administrator questions classroom management because students appear too noisy and unfocused	Mentor intervenes to reframe for the administrator student engagement; continues to build student inquiry into lesson design
3	Serene	Kurt's comments about the reading being "words on a page" reflect confusion about how a gender critical theory would apply to a text without female identifying characters	Rehearses ways of reteaching critical lens with different texts
4-5	Alexandra	"Pulling teeth" during discussion when no one appears willing to talk	Rehearses new ways of interacting with students; ways of explicitly teaching students how to participate in discussion, including clarifying the purposes for discussion in her classroom
5	Darius and colleagues	Referring to students as "my besties" to make them feel included as a part of the classroom community	Reconsidering how to communicate to students that we as teachers want them to feel a sense of welcome and belonging in our classrooms
6-8	Natalie	What to do when a student shares disparaging comments and uncertainty about engaging in conversations about texts that include the lived experiences of those who identify differently than social or community norms	Rehearse ways of teaching students how to engage in class discussion, even when they may not agree with a viewpoint or perspective offered; rehearse next steps for teaching content that will widen students' understanding about populations which have historically been subjugated or made invisible in the school or curricula
6-8	Amelie	A mentor teacher who is reticent to allow curricular change because of department and school norms and policies	Negotiate an "experiment" lesson
7	Martha	A mentor teacher's banking framework supports an approach to discussion that centers the teacher's voice	Rehearsing ways of teaching students how to engage in dialogic interactions and discussion
7	Darby	A student's obsession with grades as a byproduct of the systems of schooling he's grown up in	Continue revisiting the relationship between assessment and grading with students
8	Jess	Even though students buy into a mentor teacher's framework that emphasizes the value of college readiness, they need support for learning the literacy skills needed to succeed in college	Infuse modeling into lesson instruction that aligns with mentor teacher's framework and department curriculum

Figure 9.1 Case teachers action summary

in lesson design and interactions with others, space to rehearse possibilities for future instructional choices, places to invite others to offer us feedback on our efforts, and rethinking language choices as we seek to position students as agentive knowers and doers. That each took some form of action seems a foregone response to emergent sticking points. After all, as we've seen, each teacher learned about their sticking point while engaged in the negotiation process. What they learned undoubtedly informed their decision-making about how to respond.

Choosing Action

Engaging the process of negotiation and, therefore, choosing when to act after reframing follows no prescriptive timeline. A teacher might engage in the negotiation process for minutes, days, weeks, or a whole semester. A lot depends upon the interactions, the people involved, the timing, the context, the system, and so on. But no matter the timeline, all teachers make decisions to act. What's less obvious when studying Figure 9.1 is that after reframing their sticking points with the benefit of what they had learned, these teachers first had to decide *when* to act.

Sometimes it makes sense for teachers to act immediately. That is, they can put into action a plan for navigating or responding to the sticking point because of what they've learned and because there is space, time, and strength of relational support from others (e.g., mentors, field instructors, administrators, families) to do so.

Other times, though, a teacher may, after weighing what they have learned, decide not to take immediate action in response to a sticking point. In these cases, a teacher may determine that it's best to carry on. For pre-service teachers, especially, who are guests in the classrooms of mentors and host schools, carrying on may mean not intervening at all in the space and time of those relationships. Instead, it may mean internalizing and benefitting from what they've learned and using that knowledge to inform ongoing interactions. That choice may at times feel like one has to choose to give up on their framework commitments, to sell out, if you will. But a choice to not take immediate action reflects a critical ability to discern where we can affect the greatest change. Sometimes a choice to wait can open possibilities for future action that leads to more sustainable, long-term change, as we'll explore shortly.

No matter whether a teacher chooses to take immediate action or carry on with the benefit of new insights, all socially just ELA teachers reflect on, rehearse, and contemplate how what they've learned will inform future instructional interactions—whether in the same classrooms, schools, and districts or not. This forward action is critically important to learning from ongoing efforts to negotiate sticking points. In the sections that follow, we'll delve deeper into what it means and what we consider when we decide to act now, not act in the moment, and act forward.

Acting Now

After reframing sticking points, teachers identify where openings exist for action. To further concretize how these openings become visible to them, let's examine the openings that some of the case teachers identified (see Figure 9.2). As they searched for openings, these teachers did not feel they had to compromise their commitment to socially just ELA instruction. They definitely had to adapt and adjust. By looking for places where they could work with others' framework commitments and investments to find alignment and opportunity to work together, though, they found spaces to enact their commitments without compromising their relationship with others, including especially mentors and students in the classrooms where they worked.

The teacher's ability to lookout for three kinds of interconnected openings supported their ability to discover and, at times, create opportunities where they may not have been immediately visible.

Small Experiments

For many of the case teachers, an opportunity to teach a future lesson or portion of a lesson offered a space to negotiate a small instructional experiment where they could design and rehearse a possibility for enacting socially just ELA instruction. They discovered that a mentor might be more apt to go along with a small experiment than the suggestion of a whole new way of teaching or a new unit.

For example, after reframing her sticking point, Amelie saw that it would not be possible or advantageous for her to push forward her desire to redesign the upcoming unit of study. She understood more fully what was at stake for her mentor and that it would be nearly impossible for her to quickly jump on board plans for a reworked unit design, especially because Amelie's vision wouldn't easily align with her mentor's framework or the department's common assessment. However, Amelie thought it might be feasible to explore with her mentor teacher the possibility of an experimental lesson at the start of the unit. In that lesson, she proposed, she could try out some of her ideas for infusing a youth lens into the class conversation about the core text. She believed this lesson might engage students, because she sought to help them connect their lived experience and current events with their upcoming study

Chapter	Teacher	Reframed Sticking Point	Openings	Choices to Act Now
1	Alex	Students did not choose the "socially just" reading assessment options	Future teaching opportunities within the same and other classrooms; supportive MTs; aligned choices with department's commitment to choice reading	Revised reading assessment options for future iterations of the assignment within and across semesters
4-5	Alexandra	"Pulling teeth" during discussion when no one appears willing to talk	Ongoing opportunities to work with small groups in the same classroom; instruction aligned with MT's focus	Tried out new language for inviting student responses that enabled them to save face and share without feeling like Alexandra was fishing for "right" answers
6-8	Amelie	A mentor teacher who is reticent to allow curricular change because of department and school norms and policies	An upcoming unit where she would be the lead instructor; owning the potential for an "experiment" lesson to fail	Negotiated a single "experiment" lesson within the MT's larger unit
7	Martha	A mentor teacher's banking framework supports an approach to discussion that centers the teacher's voice	MT's invitation for Martha to facilitate discussion during a future lesson	Rehearsed ways of teaching students how to engage in dialogic interactions and discussion
8	Jess	Even though students buy into a mentor teacher's framework that emphasizes the value of college readiness, they need support for learning the literacy skills needed to succeed in college	Adopting the language of college readiness; identifying transferrable literacy skills that spoke to MT's framework	Infused modeling into lesson instruction that aligns with MT's framework and department curriculum

Figure 9.2 Case teachers acting now choices

of the text. This single lesson experiment would enable her to rehearse small-scale possibilities that she might return to and expand upon in future teaching.

As Amelie's case makes clear, negotiating small instructional experiments can be a strategic way to explore and create opportunities to enact socially just ELA instruction. What's more, Amelie thought carefully about how best to frame and approach a conversation with her mentor teacher before acting. She found herself contemplating ways of broaching the possibility with her mentor. Figure 9.3 offers some possibilities for negotiating small experiments.

- "I'm not sure if this will go as I imagine, but I'd love to be able to try out the possibility of. . . ."
- "I wonder how it might benefit student learning if in my upcoming lesson/small group/conference, I ask students/try . . ."
- "I wonder if we might explore together the possibility of . . . during. . . ."

Figure 9.3 Language for negotiating small experiments

Shared Goals

For the case teachers, another important and related opening arose from awareness of how their instructional goals might align with someone else's goals, even if they might not necessarily share framework commitments. Seeking and identifying shared goals with those mentors, students, and colleagues with whom we work can help create opportunities to work together more effectively.

Alexandra, for instance, shared her mentor's commitment to teaching students critical theory as a vehicle for helping them critically analyze representations of gender in texts, which might help build their awareness of how ideologies manifest in texts, including through character analysis. As students grappled with the application of the lens, she saw a need to reteach and adjust her approaches to facilitating discussion about the lens. She wanted to be careful about how she broached the topic of reteaching, because she did not want her mentor to think that she was suggesting that the initial lessons introducing the gender lens were insufficient. Instead, she wanted to suggest that students still needed more instruction and support as they worked to apply their understanding for the textual analysis assignment. By focusing on her shared commitment to teaching critical theory, she was able to underscore how they were aligned in their efforts to support student learning. She was careful in her conversation to try and make sure that she positioned herself and her observations in ways that messaged to her mentor that she saw them as jointly troubleshooting a sticking point that was an inevitable part of ELA teaching that seeks to respond to student need and strengths.

Alexandra's case emphasizes the value of seeking and identifying spaces where we share instructional goals so that those with whom we work see us as allies in actualizing a shared vision. It's inevitable that the ways we go about actualizing that vision or shared set of goals may differ. However, when mentors, colleagues, students, and administrators see that we share a commitment to the larger aim, it's possible to work differently together. They see us as jointly invested, and they're more likely to listen and to see our efforts as less a threat and more a concern for finding ways, often multiple, to accomplish the same end goals.

Language Cohesion

As ELA teachers, we value the rhetorically powerful ways that people use language to accomplish work and change in the world. In our work as teachers, how we use our language is an important skill set. Through their engagement in the sticking point negotiation process, especially through inquiry and radical listening, the case teachers attended carefully to the language that others in their interactions used. Understanding how others language their commitments and framework investments enabled the case teachers to identify language choices that mattered to their interactants (those they interacted with) (Beach & Beauchemin, 2019; Beach & Bloome, 2019).

Jess noticed that the language of "college readiness" was incredibly important to his mentor and the students in their classroom. It signaled a clear goal and rationale for literacy learning in the class. While Jess questioned in his notemaking whether college readiness ought to be the "be all and end all goal" of the class's learning, he couldn't deny the significance of the phrase and its exigence in the class. For Jess, college readiness was a step along a pathway toward helping students achieve not only their professional goals but also find joy and seek justice in their worlds. If, he surmised, adopting the language of "college readiness" would signal to his mentor and students that he shared their vision, he might find openings and opportunities to support that goal and extend it in showing students glimpses of other possibilities for their literacy learning, too. Adopting "college readiness," then wasn't inauthentic or disingenuous for Jess. It was a rhetorically savvy way to align himself with his mentor and create openings for instructional experimentation.

In Jess and other case examples, we see how finding openings is a direct response to what teachers learn as they engage in the negotiation process.

Deciding Not to Act Now

For some teachers, it is surprising to learn that a choice to not act can feel as empowering as a choice to act. Yet, a decision not to act—at least right away—is a form of action. A discerning decision not to act often results from growing awareness of interactional dynamics, including who holds power.

There are times, especially for beginning teachers, when choosing to take action may create more sticking points than one has space, time, and power to effectively negotiate. In these cases, choosing not to act may be more advantageous than choosing to act, especially when taking action might damage a relationship with someone in a position of power (e.g., a mentor or a field instructor) who plays a pivotal role in a teacher's future professional progress. There may also be times when a teacher determines they don't have sufficient time to ethically be present to help negotiate the effects of their actions. Take the case of Marco, a teacher candidate, who saw the need to open space for a conversation about race in a classroom where his mentor chose to sidestep it in their study of *Huckleberry Finn* (Twain et al., 2003/1985/1885).

☞ 9.1 Marco, in his own words

Oh man, it was killing me to know that my mentor was totally avoiding a meaningful conversation about race. How can you teach *Huck Finn* and not talk about race? I kept asking in my field log and in the car ride home with my colleague.

But, you know, the tension for me was that I knew conversations about race, especially in this white middle-class suburban classroom, would need to be scaffolded. Students needed to be taught how to engage in conversations about race so that they could participate effectively and deeply.

I mean, let's face it, I was also aware that I was a brown Latino male in a predominately white suburban classroom. There was so much at stake for me in raising the question with my mentor, let alone the class.

I also knew that this unit began two weeks before my involvement in the class was set to end. I had already taught, and my mentor hadn't mentioned that I could teach another lesson during this unit. It was pretty clear that I was supposed to soak it all in.

I decided to do nothing, which at the time felt like failure to stand up for what I believe socially just ELA teaching should be about. I had failed. I had sidestepped race talk, too.

But, later after processing with my colleagues, I realize that I couldn't have done what I had hoped to accomplish in such a short period. And, actually, stepping in could have caused more harm than good in the end.

For Marco, a choice to not take action weighed heavily on his mind. He shared this reflection weeks after he had left this classroom, so it's clear he was unsettled. Nonetheless, it's important to understand the evolution of Marco's reflection about the sticking point, which he begins to touch on with his comments about how difficult it would have been for him to affect and enact the change to which he has so deeply committed: teaching students how to engage in explicit conversations about race as they talk about texts (Kay, 2018; Schieble et al., 2020; Thomas, 2015). Opening the conversation without support or shared understanding from a mentor teacher who may have felt obliged or, perhaps, ill-prepared to continue the conversation once Marco left, may have risked further alienating some students or exacerbating social rifts in the class dynamic, say nothing of what it could mean for Marco's relationship with those students and others in the school building with whom he knew he might have future interactions during student teaching. These are the complex dynamics that engaging the negotiation process enables us to navigate. As Marco's case makes clear, choosing not to act can be a nerve-wracking decision. But as Marco's colleagues and field instructor emphasized for him, his decision was informed by a host of understandings about the interactional dynamics at play in his sticking point. His decision was also informed by his limited power to meaningfully affect change in the space of the classroom and school, especially as a visiting teacher candidate.

Marco is not alone. Some of the teachers in the cases we've already met also chose to not take immediate action. After reframing their sticking points and weighing whether there were openings for action, these teachers discerned that it might be best to not take further action. Figure 9.4 offers specifics about why each teacher chose not to act.

There was no personal failure in these teachers' choices not to act, because they had solid and reasonable logic informing those decisions. It wasn't at all as if they threw their hands up and said essentially, "I give up. This is too complicated." On the contrary, their understanding of interactional, classroom culture, school systems, and ELA content and pedagogy dynamics all informed their choices.

Inquiry and Listening as Action

Moreover, it's important to remember that even though these teachers decided not to take immediate action after reframing and reanalyzing the sticking points they faced, many had already positively intervened. As they inquired to learn more and radically listen, they were assuming an agentive, action-oriented stance. Take, for example, Serene's case. In her interactions with Kurt, she asked him to read aloud a passage from his book so that she could learn more about how he was making meaning of the text as he read. She was informally assessing and seeking to understand his comments about "words on the page." By doing so, she communicated to Kurt that she took his comment seriously. She took him seriously as a learner. She cared and wanted to understand so that she could identify how to respond. In a world

Chapter	Teacher	Reframed Sticking Point	Logic for Choosing Not to Act Now
2	Cruz	Administrator questions classroom management because students appear too noisy and unfocused	Mentor intervened to reframe for the administrator student engagement; Cruz didn't feel the need to interject, especially because he learned of the exchange between his MT and administrator afterward
3	Serene	Kurt's comments about the reading being "words on a page" reflect confusion about how a gender critical theory would apply to a text without female identifying characters	During the inquiry process, Kurt adjusted his application of the lens during his conversation with students. Serene felt she needed more time to see how Kurt would continue (or not) in this line of thinking before taking further action.
5	Darius and colleagues	Referring to students as "my besties" to make them feel included as a part of the classroom community	Darius only came to learn of the sticking point after the fact and after he had stopped his clinical work
6-8	Natalie	What to do when a student shares disparaging comments and uncertainty about engaging in conversations about texts that include the lived experiences of those who identify differently than social or community norms	Natalie felt she needed to learn more about how her MT might advise intervening in the conversation, especially because Natalie did not want to risk her MT's ability to teach gender and queer theory in the school
7	Darby	A student's obsession with grades as a byproduct of the systems of schooling he's grown up in	Darby felt that students would benefit from an ongoing conversation, as she realized she could not dictate that students adopt a new framework for assessment just because she said so; she believed navigating the sticking point would require a "slow brew" approach; she didn't want to discount students' questions and uncertainty either

Figure 9.4 Case teachers choosing not to act

where so many adolescents feel overlooked and misunderstood, Serene's efforts to pause, inquire, and listen were a positive intervention. As a result, Kurt revisited his reading and efforts to apply the lens to his analysis. He tried again and showed Serene that he might in fact understand more than he let on with his earliest comments.

In other words, engaging in sticking point negotiation is a form of action. That negotiation process reveals next steps. Sometimes we see space for immediate next steps, and at other points, we may not or we may determine that acting immediately may do more harm than good. It's important to remember, too, that it's impractical to assume that we will be able to act immediately on every sticking point that emerges. In fact, to take immediate action in response to every sticking point that we notice might indicate that we're not fully embracing the process of negotiation.

Seeing Momentary Inaction as a Part of Commitment to Long-Term Action

Perhaps you know people who pick up every fad that comes their way. They've always got the latest, greatest. After a while, you might wonder, who are they really? What are they really committed to? What grounds their decision-making?

Reminding ourselves of what matters by continually returning to and revising our socially just ELA framework can ground us in the difficult and complex decisions about whether (or not) to take action. If we wish to be able to stay the course, to remain committed to socially just ELA instruction and the requisite work that entails of being able to work in rhetorically savvy ways within systems of inequity, then our long-term vision can help settle us when we feel we are compromising those commitments because we see it is impractical or too risky to take immediate action.

Acting Forward

In the previous section, I was careful to emphasize how the teachers chose not to take *immediate* or in-the-moment action after reframing their sticking points. I did so to highlight that a choice not to take immediate action does not indicate that these teachers weren't simultaneously looking toward and rehearsing future action. Every single one of them, whether they found opportunities for immediate action or not, was concurrently reflecting on how what they'd learned would inform their future instructional decision-making. While we all know that the exact particulars of sticking points may not recur in our future teaching, it's highly likely that we'll need to navigate similar dynamics.

So what, then, do we take away from sticking point negotiation, even when we decide not to take immediate action? Engaging in the ongoing practice of sticking point negotiation, including reflecting on and rehearsing possibilities for future action is a lot like physical conditioning. As someone who needs special motivation and incentive to workout, my more athletically inclined and adept family and friends remind me that the more we exercise, the easier and more fluid it becomes. The more adaptable and responsive our bodies become to the unexpected. But, also, when we keep the practice and conditioning process in-motion, we feel better prepared to respond in the future. Research affirms that maintaining our conditioning practice yields long term health and wellness benefits. Negotiating sticking points, no matter the ultimate outcome, is similar. We need to maintain our engagement in the process to continue to benefit from it in the long-term.

Maintaining an eye on the future, then, is a critical part of choosing to act in response to sticking points, and there are many ways to maintain this vision, as the cases we've already met make clear in Figure 9.5.

Some important themes emerge by studying the choices the case teachers chose in their efforts to act forward:

- Revisiting previous learning about ELA content, pedagogy, instructional processes;
- Consulting trusted professionals who can advise us about instructional possibilities, including mentors, colleagues, former instructors, department or program leadership, and professional organizations;
- Researching and tracking the latest research and pedagogical practices in peer-reviewed journals, professional publications, and through attendance at conferences and other events to network with other ELA teachers and instructional leaders;
- Rehearsing possibilities with others who can provide constructive feedback about ideas in progress or lesson design, which will help revise and fine-tune before teaching or planning further; and
- Redesigning instruction with the benefit of ongoing learning.

Our efforts to act forward help us maintain an active stance toward our teaching, and importantly, ongoing professional learning. These efforts also maintain our engagement in the recursive process of sticking point negotiation. When we make a decision to act or not, we begin the cycle again, aware that future sticking points will emerge. Yet, we can rest assured that our engagement in the full process, including in choosing how to act and when to act, will lead to clarity about future decision-making and responsiveness. Forward acting helps us rehearse explanations for why certain instructional choices matter to us and how they benefit student learning in our future classes.

 9.2 Reflecting

Revisit your thinking in box 8.5. Or choose one of the sticking points that has emerged for you more recently in your fieldwork. How has or is your negotiation of that sticking point revealing to you possibilities for acting forward on what you've learned? If possible, share your thinking with a trusted colleague or mentor to gather feedback or, possibly, to expand the possibilities of your own thinking forward.

Chapter	Teacher	Reframed Sticking Point	Acting Forward
1	Alex	Students did not choose the "socially just" reading assessment options	Revises reading assessment options for future iterations of the assignment
2	Cruz	Administrator questions classroom management because students appear too noisy and unfocused	Continues to build student inquiry into lesson design; rehearses with MT how student engagement can align with administrators' focus on classroom management, so he has ways of explaining it to future administrators or colleagues
3	Serene	Kurt's comments about the reading being "words on a page" reflect confusion about how a gender critical theory would apply to a text without female identifying characters	Researches ways of reteaching critical lens with different texts; rehearses these possibilities with her field instructor and colleagues; tries these ideas out in her course unit plan
4-5	Alexandra	"Pulling teeth" during discussion when no one appears willing to talk	Rehearses new ways of interacting with students, including ways of explicitly teaching students how to participate in discussion; asks mentors and other advisors for resources to support her professional inquiry in this area
5	Darius and colleagues	Referring to students as "my besties" to make them feel included as a part of the classroom community	Reconsiders how to signal to students a sense of welcome and belonging in his classroom; rehearses possibilities and reflects on them in future teaching in different clinical classrooms; creates a field log section to specifically catalogue language that accomplishes this goal
6-8	Natalie	What to do when a student shares disparaging comments and uncertainty about engaging in conversations about texts that include the lived experiences of those who identify differently than social or community norms	Rehearses ways of teaching students how to engage in class discussion, even when they may not agree with a viewpoint or perspective offered; researches next steps for teaching content that will widen students' understanding about populations which have historically been subjugated or made invisible in the school or curricula; subscribes to professional journals, joins organizations, and begins following digital resources to stay abreast of current conversations among other ELA teachers and researchers so that she can advocate for these approaches in her future teaching

Figure 9.5 Case teachers acting forward *(Continued)*

6-8	Amelie	A mentor teacher who is reticent to allow curricular change because of department and school norms and policies	Negotiates an "experiment" lesson; reflects with her field instructor and mentor using student data from and responses to the lesson; solicits further research and resources for building her knowledge about the youth lens for future teaching
7	Martha	A mentor teacher's banking framework supports an approach to discussion that centers the teacher's voice	Rehearses ways of teaching students how to engage in dialogic interactions and discussion with the help of her field instructor, former instructors, and colleagues
8	Jess	Even though students buy into a mentor teacher's framework that emphasizes the value of college readiness, they need support for learning the literacy skills needed to succeed in college	Infuses modeling into lesson instruction that aligns with MT's framework and department curriculum; reflects in field log on the effectiveness of these efforts, including how she might plan this work across a semester-long course rather than in short, disconnected lessons

Figure 9.5 *(Continued)*

References

Beach, R., & Beauchemin, F. (2019). *Teaching language as action in the ELA classroom.* Routledge.

Beach, R., & Bloome, D. (Eds.). (2019). *Languaging relations for transforming the literacy and language arts classroom.* Routledge.

Kay, M. R. (2018). *Not light, but fire: How to lead meaningful race conversations in the classroom.* Stenhouse.

Schieble, M., Vetter, A., & Monét, K. (2020). *Classroom talk for social change: Critical conversations in English language arts.* Teachers College Press.

Thomas, E. E. (2015). "We always talk about race": Navigating race talk dilemmas in the teaching of literature. *Research in the Teaching of English, 50*(2), 154–175

Twain, M., Seelye, J., & Cardwell, G. (2003/1985/1885). *The adventures of Huckleberry Finn.* Penguin Classics.

10

Journeying Together

As Lena neared the end of her student teaching experience, she reflected on how much she had come to value the sticking point negotiation process. To her surprise, though, embracing the process had also revealed a connected sticking point. As she prepared to transition to a new classroom space—her own classroom in a new school and district, she wondered:

☞ **10.1 Lena, in her own words**

Both my biggest goal and my biggest sticking point at this point is, "How do you continue this work?" I feel like this is a "lifestyle" to live in as a teacher. Lifestyles take time to develop and as a new teacher I feel like I don't have all the resources and experience necessary to continue this work. When I get stuck, I'm worried that I will fall back into my own experiences of schooling or what teachers around me suggest rather than staying true to my commitments to socially just English language arts (ELA) instruction.

DOI: 10.4324/9781003134442-13

Lena worried about losing her ability to engage the process. At the same time, she understood that sticking point negotiation is an ongoing process that benefits from continual revisiting and recommitment. The fact that she was aware of her own uncertainty but also reassured by her knowledge that negotiation is an ongoing professional way of being suggests that Lena may well have been farther along in her ability to sustain the process in her future teaching than she may have realized. Lena's comments reveal her implicit realization that sustaining the process in her professional life would benefit from a community of colleagues. As she reflected on her relationship with her mentor teacher, she noted:

 10.2 Lena, in her own words

I appreciated her balance between treating me like a colleague and understanding that I am a new teacher. She was respectful. She shared her ideas while also being comfortable totally backing off and allowing me to lesson plan however I wanted. That gave me confidence to take risks, knowing that she would help me process and negotiate sticking points that might result.

For Lena, reflecting on this relationship gave her a vision of the kinds of collegial and mentoring relationships she wanted to continue to seek and foster in her future teaching life. Because she valued her experience in her mentor teacher's classroom, she knew that she would want to find and contribute to a network of teachers who valued similar ways of inquiring and learning together as an inherent part of maintaining and evolving their commitment to socially just ELA instruction.

Inquiry Communities

Lena's reflections affirm the importance of community in sustaining our efforts to enact socially just ELA instruction within the contexts where we work but also in relationship with other teachers beyond our immediate space. As Darius's experiences (see Chapters Five and Nine) contemplating "besties" remind us, too, ongoing inquiry conversations with colleagues can continue to support and bolster our ability to see sticking points that might otherwise remain invisible to us. Where we identify sticking points, colleagues can be instrumental in helping us negotiate sticking points, especially with the benefit their insider and outsider perspectives, as we discussed in Chapter Two.

Cam and Glenda: Case Study

The value of insider and outsider perspectives became critical to the community that Cam and Glenda, two veteran teachers who work in an urban high school, contributed to as they worked together and with department colleagues to enact a new curriculum. Cam and Glenda had worked together for over ten years, and each had been teaching ELA for over 15 years.

Their public high school served a predominately Black student population from a set of low-income neighborhoods. Many students chose to open-enroll in the high school, because of its close proximity to the urban core with a much larger school district. Families appreciated the smaller school size and the stronger academic reputation.

Cam and Glenda agreed to pilot a new curriculum that Cam had been a part of developing the year before. The curriculum was focused on helping students develop their argumentative writing skills. Cam and Glenda saw their involvement in a larger pilot with other regional schools as an opportunity to strengthen their own writing instruction. The curriculum itself was designed to be highly scaffolded. The goal? To enable teachers to help students see how what they learn to do in each lesson builds from the previous lesson and ultimately supports their ability to write an essay by the end of the unit.

Cam and Glenda met regularly to co-observe each other's teaching and debrief emergent sticking points as they worked to implement and adjust the curriculum in their classes. On this Monday, they are meeting to discuss one of Glenda's classes that Cam had observed the Friday before. As they open their conversation, Cam invites Glenda to begin by sharing what is on her mind. Glenda explains how things went in class that day, and that update includes the emergence of a sticking point: her students have not progressed in the unit work as quickly as she and Cam had planned.

GLENDA: Ok. So, we know what the attendance situation is around here. What happened today in both classes is if students weren't here Friday to write their claim and to start pulling some evidence to start supporting their claim from the articles, it messed them up for today. They were *not* able to do the assignment.

CAM: Absolutely. Right.

GLENDA: So that was a *big* thing. And so, *this* [points to the graphic organizers from Friday's lesson] was overwhelming enough, but then there's always this subgroup in each class where they're like, "I don't even." They don't even have a claim yet. They didn't have a claim. They didn't have evidence. So, I'm trying to help some students with today's lesson and some with Friday's lesson, of course. I would try to say to some of the students who were here on Friday, "Can you try to help show [those who were absent] what you did Friday?"

CAM: How did that work?

GLENDA: Um [laughs], better in first hour than in second hour.

CAM: Okay

GLENDA: Because the second thing that happened is even if they were here on Friday, many didn't finish the assignment, which I kind of anticipated in some cases. I said, "You can take your folder home to finish." But then they came back today, and they still hadn't identified evidence, or they left their folder at home, or they clearly didn't do anything on Friday or the weekend, so they also were behind.

CAM: Yeah

GLENDA: So that was a huge group of students.

CAM: Yeah

GLENDA: So, then when we started today with so many who hadn't finished this packet, even if they were working pretty hard, it took a while for most of them to get between two and three paragraphs. So, I made them a deal. I said, "Okay. I could extend this to two days, because you didn't have the time to do it. *But* then you have to come back on Tuesday and be able to write about what we've been working on." They were begging me, "Please, can we work on this tomorrow?" So, I folded on that, and I said, "Okay, we'll do this for two days," because there were all these other people who needed to get caught up. And then we'll do the flash draft on a Wednesday rather than tomorrow, which I know the reasons why it might be a bad idea.

CAM: Well, but let's talk about why it *might* work, because I'm thinking about if these graphic organizers were well put together, especially if you gave students an extension, then they *are* the essay that students need to write, you know?

GLENDA: Yep. They are. That's why they're having a hard time grasping I think that we're doing this step by step, the scaffolding of different *skills* one at a time. I'm trying to explain to them, "Okay, this one page is a paragraph and another paragraph and another one."

CAM: So, it's the first time through this process, yes?

GLENDA: Yes, first time through this process is a little, you know. I'm trying. I'm working at it.

CAM: Exactly.

Glenda's sticking point is one that Cam can appreciate for a few related reasons. First, as Glenda alludes to right away, Cam understands student attendance patterns, because she, too, teaches in the building. It's a problem that the school and district are working on, but it presents challenges in their joint efforts to keep their unit instruction moving forward while catching up students who have been absent—in some cases, for long periods of time—so that everyone can progress in their learning and writing. It's notable that on other occasions the two have talked about how their efforts to implement this unit are considered "counterculture" in their school, because, as they describe it, "teachers often slow instruction down so much because of absence, that they never really get anywhere." In fact, there's lots of conversation within the school about attendance patterns since students habitually underperform on state mandated and standardized assessment measures.

Second, because Cam is also implementing and adjusting the unit, she understands the curricular goals well and can quickly join Glenda in the particulars of the lessons that she's referencing. She knows what they aim to accomplish in each lesson as well as the intent of the provided instructional supports (e.g., graphic organizers).

Third, they share a commitment to socially just ELA instruction. On the surface, their discussion of this sticking point may not immediately make evident their efforts to enact this curriculum as a part of their commitment to social justice. However, Cam and Glenda both see students' growing ability to write effective arguments as central to supporting students' ability to advocate for change in their lives and communities. For both teachers who live in the same community, teaching students how their writing can affect social change is a way of disrupting deficit ideologies that pervade local, state, and national conversations about urban teenagers and cities. They seek to affirm students' ability to use their literacy skills to create different possibilities for their futures and for the future of their communities. An issue like attendance, for them, and being able to move forward with the curricular goals they've set for themselves are intimately related to teaching for justice. The sticking point Glenda raises, then, and their ability to jointly negotiate it have implications for both teachers, their students, and their department, because their colleagues are eagerly watching what they can make possible through their curricular pilot efforts.

Cam's ability to negotiate the sticking point with Glenda on this day and across time speaks to the power of collegial community in supporting and sustaining the work of socially just ELA instruction. Together, throughout this exchange, we see evidence of their eagerness to embrace the negotiation process. Glenda frames the sticking point. She offers observations from her inquiry and radical listening. And when she jumps to the conclusion that her decision to extend Monday's lesson a couple of days is a "bad idea," Cam interjects to take stock and reframe the sticking point. She suggests that perhaps it's not a "bad idea" at all to take a bit more time, because doing so will help all students develop their essay drafts as they complete the graphic organizers. Whereas Glenda initially sees her "giving in" to students' desires to extend the lesson as antithetical to their joint instructional efforts, Cam suggests in her response that her action may in fact be aligned with their shared goals and framework. Rather than attendance issues, the sticking point, as Cam reframes it may be more about how best to, within the realities that they're both navigating, support students in accomplishing the unit goals by helping them complete, eventually, the summative assessment. As a result of her reframing, Cam affirms Glenda's action: to extend the instruction for now. Beyond that, Cam reminds Glenda that it's everyone's first time through the unit, and there's reason to allow themselves to be responsive to student needs.

Not long after in their conversation, Cam helps Glenda navigate a related sticking point: how to help students take the leap and begin drafting so that they can complete their "quick write." Cam rehearses with Glenda a possible way of framing the "fast draft" work for students when she revisits what's next on Tuesday in class:

☞ **10.3 Cam, in her own words**

So, when you sit down and draft, you'll have everything you need. You have your notebook. You have this graphic organizer. You have that graphic organizer. So, you'll make lots of decisions Wednesday about putting the writing together and trying to make it make sense. It's a fast draft, not a final draft. This is your moment to put it all together as best you can. Here's the resources you have, and you can make it come together. If all you have is your mind, and your articles, and your lined paper, then that's what you can use.

After pausing, Cam offers a suggestion for Glenda that derives from her experiences developing the unit with teachers from other schools as much as it is a check to make sure they're on the same page:

☞ **10.4 Cam, in her own words**

I like that you extended today's lesson an extra day, but I'd warn against extending the draft an extra day. We need to see what students can come up with initially in that timeframe of a single lesson so that we know how to adjust our revision instruction and workshop lessons. We'll see the difference between the kids who have no scaffolds, right, like these graphic organizers versus the kids who do. We'll see how these lessons we're teaching with the graphic organizers make a difference or not, and that will be so helpful to us in moving forward with this group and in future semesters.

In these comments, Cam is reiterating that they're both engaged in shared and important instructional inquiry. Proceeding in the unit will help students move forward, but it will also help them reassess their own teaching and adjust as they go. It will help them respond to their students' needs and strengths as emerging writers. Thus, Cam proposes that they recommit to their "fast draft" action plan.

This exchange between Cam and Glenda reveals the power of collegial community in negotiating sticking points but also, when our inquiry and listening suggest, staying the course by persisting in our commitments and plans—not blindly, of course, but after continually engaging in the process together with others who can serve as thinking partners and critical inquirers with us. Even with their more than 15 years of teaching experience, Cam and Glenda remind us that teaching offers few clear "solutions" to sticking points. Without a community of colleagues with whom we can pose sticking points, grapple, inquire, listen, wonder, reframe, act, and reflect, we may second guess our best intentions and our commitment to socially just instruction. Worse yet, we risk giving up on these commitments all together.

Sustaining Your Commitment to Socially Just ELA Instruction

Communities of colleagues sustain our efforts, but they also reinvigorate our enthusiasm for the joyful complexity and intellectual challenge of teaching, especially for those of us who understand the critical need to responsively navigate and negotiate sticking points. Cam and Glenda offer us a vision of what's possible when veteran teachers benefit from generative collaboration that helps them negotiate sticking points.

Maximizing the Benefits of Your Collegial Inquiry Communities

Let's concretize what it is about the collaborative, inquiry-driven negotiations that Cam, Glenda, and the other teachers you've met on the pages of this book found meaningfully sustaining:

- They **share** basic **framework orientations and commitments to socially just ELA instruction**, even if they use different language or framework names.
- They **jointly engage in the negotiation of sticking points** that emerge organically in their teaching and professional interactions.
- They **see sticking points as resources** for growing their practice and deepening their understanding of how to support all students' learning within the classrooms and schools where they work and learn.
- Their **ongoing professional learning is driven by inquiry** into and a desire to negotiate sticking points, especially those that help them teach for justice.
- They believe that **mutually supporting one another's negotiation benefits everyone** in that community, because any chance to talk through the negotiation practice in relation to the context where it emerges helps everyone involved reflect on their own practice and interactions.
- They **offer alternate interpretations, or framing, of sticking points** to help each other consider and reconsider "what's going on."
- They **focus on specifics** (e.g., student data, the language of teaching a particular lesson or interaction) to situate their notetaking, notemaking, and perspectives.
- They **wonder together**. They ask questions about what they are noticing.
- They **radically listen** to one another, to students, and to what's going on in their context.
- They **explore possibilities** made visible through the reframing of sticking points.
- They help each other **consider whether, when, and what action to take** as a result of what they learn and navigate together.
- They **reflect on their action** in light of what they've learned and where they're headed in support of student learning and student ability to transfer their learning to their lives and world needs—local and beyond.

 10.5 Reflecting

Reflect on your experiences with collegial communities. In what ways, if any, where they spaces where you could find support for sticking point negotiation? As you move forward, what can you do to foster collegial communities that support your own and others' sticking point negotiation? How might you

- invite others into that negotiation work?
- use what you've learned to explain the benefits of mutual support of that negotiation work?
- grow your collective understanding of the process for negotiating sticking points?

Building and Nurturing Your Sustainable Network for Radical Possibilities

Even with this vision of what's possible, seeking communities of inquiry that can sustain our commitment and efforts to enact socially just ELA instruction can feel challenging. Many of the pre-service teachers who you've met on the pages of this book began fostering and contributing to a community of like-minded and committed colleagues, mentors, or field instructors during fieldwork. After that work is complete transitioning into a new school community can present its own kind of sticking point, as Trey reflected just before he began his first teaching job:

☞ **10.6 Trey, in his own words**

Honestly, the main sticking point I have about enacting socially just ELA instruction is determining how "radical" I will be when I enter the profession. Up to this point in my journey to become an ELA teacher, I have become the voice for the movement and have given away a lot of myself when pushing back. Though I am not drowning in a sea of rage–I really like this work, I have concerns about burning out or being so radical that I will possibly be removed from the classroom.

Implicit in Trey's comments is an understanding that when teachers enter a new teaching context, they may find themselves dropped into an ineffective system. The conditions may not be ideal. If you think of yourself in Trey's position as someone also committed to socially just ELA instruction as well as to affecting positive change through your day-to-day teaching and professional interactions, you may feel like you're an outlier, if the community you enter is not well matched with your framework orientations.

Trey's not alone in his worry about feeling too "radical" for the "real world" he's about to enter. However, the visions of possibility that Cam and Glenda and the other teachers you've met offer underscores the value of seeking, finding, and, at times, fostering a community of inquiry that can sustain you in the work. Just as you'll want the students in your classroom to understand and live, fostering and contributing to communities of inquiry is an essential part of continuing to learn, grow, and co-construct a different future. Students and teachers alike, we all need communities.

The professional community you foster and contribute to can become a space of radical possibility. You can create your community by finding another teacher at your school or beyond who can become a collaborative sticking point negotiator with you. Or it might be networking with those you have already established connections. At times, talking across contexts can provide a safe space to process candidly, especially as an early career or new teacher where the stakes of talking vulnerably about sticking points can feel risky until you know more about others' frameworks for teaching and teaching ELA for justice in your school or department. No matter, clarity about what makes a community effective, especially a community that can sustain your commitment and process for negotiating sticking points, can affirm what you're searching for as much as what you're also simultaneously seeking to foster and invite through your own negotiations no matter where you teach and learn.

For a book focused on learning a process for negotiating sticking points to end in a neat and tidy package with the suggestion that sticking points somehow go away would be misleading. To be sure, understanding that sticking points are a natural and normal part of the process means you will see them. In fact, you'll likely gravitate toward them, because you understand their potential for transforming your teaching and professional interactions. That you notice them speaks to the power and depth of your understanding that socially just ELA instruction is complex and messy, yes, even radical. But it's also the possibility that drives us forward and reminds us that we cannot go it alone. To understand socially just ELA instruction and what it means and looks like in practice means embracing the fact that it is impossible to sustain those efforts on our own over the long haul. Negotiating sticking points, because it is interactional work, can only be sustained with support of another or others who can check us in our seas of rage and remind us that we cannot be a voice of one. Our negotiation efforts are stronger and more enduring in the company of a collective.

Index

Note: Italicized page numbers refer to figures. Page numbers followed by "n" refer to notes.

133–137; interpretation 127–139; uncovering opportunities 133; *see also* framing
Ribay, R. 66n1

Salinger, J. D.: *Catcher in the Rye* 107, 113
Sarigianides, S. T. 66n1
shared goals 148–149
social injustice 9; response determination, resources for 8–9
socially just: definition of 33
socially just ELA instruction: centering language 35; choice reading assignment 4–5; and ethnographic method, combining 60–62; frameworks, as compasses 21–44; framing 67–80; inquiring 81–92; insider/outsider positions 38–39; lens 15; naming 112–125; noticing dissonance 55–59; opportunities for negotiation 42–44; pedagogical framework for 31–37, *32, 36*; radical listening 93–111; reframing 127–139; resources for enacting 3–18; sticking points *see* sticking points; stock, taking 112–125; sustaining the commitment to 163–166; taking action 143–156; working frameworks 35–37, *36; see also individual entries*
social power 13–14
sticking points 3–18, 40–42, 141, 158–159; case study 9–12; contextual applicability 14–15; everyday, seeing 59–60; framing, tools for 69; interlude 7–8; interpretation, impact of framework lenses on 75–77;

navigating 21–44, 45–48; negotiating 45–48; interactive process for *47*; transferrable framework for 13; professional learning, generative resources for 5–7; response determination, resources for 8–9; social and interactional power to affect change 13–14
stock, taking 112–125, 135; hearing and learning 113–114; systems considerations 124–125; zooming out 114–119, *115, 116*
sustainable network for radical possibilities, building and nurturing 165–166
systemic inequity 4, 5, 33
systems of inequity 1, 2, 23, 51, 124, 125, 153

taking action 143–156, *144*; acting forward 153–154, *155–156*; acting now 146–148, *147*; choosing action 145–146; deciding not to act now 149–153, *152*; inquiry and listening as action 151–153; language cohesion 149; momentary inaction as part of commitment to long-term action, seeing 153; shared goals 148–149; small experiments 146–147, *148*
teaching frameworks: emergence of 26; evolution of 26
Thomas, A.: *Hate U Give, The* 5
tough texts 9, 11
Twain, M.: *Huckleberry Finn* 150

zooming in 16, 88, 129, 133
zooming out 16–17, 114–116, *115, 116*, 125; case study 116–119